Kashmir

WORLD BIBLIOGRAPHICAL SERIES

General Editors:
Robert G. Neville (Executive Editor)
John J. Horton

Robert A. Myers   Hans H. Wellisch
Ian Wallace   Ralph Lee Woodward, Jr.

John J. Horton is Deputy Librarian of the University of Bradford and was formerly Chairman of its Academic Board of Studies in Social Sciences. He has maintained a longstanding interest in the discipline of area studies and its associated bibliographical problems, with special reference to European Studies. In particular he has published in the field of Icelandic and of Yugoslav studies, including the two relevant volumes in the World Bibliographical Series.

Robert A. Myers is Associate Professor of Anthropology in the Division of Social Sciences and Director of Study Abroad Programs at Alfred University, Alfred, New York. He has studied post-colonial island nations of the Caribbean and has spent two years in Nigeria on a Fulbright Lectureship. His interests include international public health, historical anthropology and developing societies. In addition to *Amerindians of the Lesser Antilles: a bibliography* (1981), *A Resource Guide to Dominica, 1493-1986* (1987) and numerous articles, he has compiled the World Bibliographical Series volumes on *Dominica* (1987), *Nigeria* (1989) and *Ghana* (1991).

Ian Wallace is Professor of German at the University of Bath. A graduate of Oxford in French and German, he also studied in Tübingen, Heidelberg and Lausanne before taking teaching posts at universities in the USA, Scotland and England. He specializes in contemporary German affairs, especially literature and culture, on which he has published numerous articles and books. In 1979 he founded the journal *GDR Monitor*, which he continues to edit under its new title *German Monitor*.

Hans H. Wellisch is Professor emeritus at the College of Library and Information Services, University of Maryland. He was President of the American Society of Indexers and was a member of the International Federation for Documentation. He is the author of numerous articles and several books on indexing and abstracting, and has published *The Conversion of Scripts and Indexing and Abstracting: an International Bibliography*, and *Indexing from A to Z*. He also contributes frequently to *Journal of the American Society for Information Science*, *The Indexer* and other professional journals.

Ralph Lee Woodward, Jr. is Director of Graduate Studies at Tulane University, New Orleans. He is the author of *Central America, a Nation Divided*, 2nd ed. (1985), as well as several monographs and more than seventy scholarly articles on modern Latin America. He has also compiled volumes in the World Bibliographical Series on *Belize* (1980), *El Salvador* (1988), *Guatemala* (Rev. Ed.) (1992) and *Nicaragua* (Rev. Ed.) (1994). Dr. Woodward edited the Central American section of the *Research Guide to Central America and the Caribbean* (1985) and is currently associate editor of Scribner's *Encyclopedia of Latin American History*.

VOLUME 225

Kashmir

David Taylor

Compiler

CLIO PRESS

OXFORD, ENGLAND · SANTA BARBARA, CALIFORNIA
DENVER, COLORADO

British Library Cataloguing in Publication Data

Taylor, David
Kashmir. – (World bibliographical series; v. 225)
1. Jammu and Kashmir (India) – Bibliography
I. Title
016.9´546

ISBN 1–85109–287–0

ABC-CLIO Ltd.,
Old Clarendon Ironworks,
35A Great Clarendon Street,
Oxford OX2 6AT, England.

———————

ABC-CLIO Inc.,
130 Cremona Drive,
Santa Barbara,
CA 93117, USA

Designed by Bernard Crossland.
Typeset by ABC-CLIO Ltd., Oxford, England.
Printed and bound in Great Britain by print in black, Midsomer Norton.

THE WORLD BIBLIOGRAPHICAL SERIES

This series, which is principally designed for the English speaker, will eventually cover every country (and some of the world's principal regions and cities), each in a separate volume comprising annotated entries on works dealing with its history, geography, economy and politics; and with its people, their culture, customs, religion and social organization. Attention will also be paid to current living conditions – housing, education, newspapers, clothing, etc. – that are all too often ignored in standard bibliographies; and to those particular aspects relevant to individual countries. Each volume seeks to achieve, by use of careful selectivity and critical assessment of the literature, an expression of the country and an appreciation of its nature and national aspirations, to guide the reader towards an understanding of its importance. The keynote of the series is to provide, in a uniform format, an interpretation of each country that will express its culture, its place in the world, and the qualities and background that make it unique. The views expressed in individual volumes, however, are not necessarily those of the publisher.

VOLUMES IN THE SERIES

Contents

Contents

Introduction

At the beginning of the 21st century, the Kashmir region has come to be associated most commonly with conflict and suffering, with terrorist actions and aircraft hijackings, with the severe abuse of human rights by security forces and with forced migration. When President Clinton, at the time of his visit to South Asia in March 2000, described the region as the most dangerous place on earth, it was Indian and Pakistani nuclear capabilities combined with the two countries' dispute over ownership of Kashmir that he had in mind. But things were not always so, even relatively recently. Until 1947, and for much of the time thereafter, the vale or valley of Kashmir was for many people the original Shangri-La, an image of peace and tranquillity. It stands on the frontiers between different cultures and, despite its apparent geographical remoteness, has been able to absorb and synthesize many different elements to form its own distinct and vibrant identity.

Kashmir as a word can refer either to the valley by itself or, as shorthand for the former 'princely state' of Kashmir, to a much larger region. This bibliography takes a maximalist approach and covers material that relates to all parts of the state as it existed from its creation in 1846, although it is now divided on a de facto basis between India and Pakistan. The total population of Indian-controlled Jammu and Kashmir is about ten million, of whom the majority live in the Kashmir valley. It is harder to estimate the population of the Pakistani-controlled areas, but the figure is probably around four million. Within the state, at least five distinct regions can be distinguished, each of which, in turn, is far from homogeneous. These regions are Kashmir, Jammu, Ladakh, the high mountains, and Azad Kashmir.

Kashmir in the restricted sense can be equated with the stretch of land where the river Jhelum broadens out into a wide valley, at an average elevation of around 5000 feet, together with the surrounding mountains. The population is predominantly Sunni Muslim, but with a culturally and politically significant Brahman Hindu minority, often known as Pandits (most of whom are currently refugees in Jammu). There are other small minorities as well. The population speaks Kashmiri, although Urdu is widely used and is, in fact, the official language. The capital of the state, Srinagar, is located in the valley. Besides the cultivation of rice, walnuts, apricots, saffron, timber and other specialist agricultural products, the valley is known for its fine shawls, carpets and papier-mâché work.

Across the Pir Panjal range of mountains in the direction of the Indian plains lies Jammu, hilly but not mountainous, and with a majority Hindu population. Culturally and linguistically, Jammu shades off into the neighbouring areas of the Punjab. Jammu City is the regional capital; the administrative capital of the state in fact shifts to Jammu during the winter months. Jammu only became closely linked with Kashmir in the 19th century, when its Dogra rulers bought Kashmir proper from the British.

To the east of the valley lies the Ladakh region, bordering on the Tibet region of China, with which it shares its Tibetan language and predominantly Buddhist culture (although there are some Shia and Sunni Muslim groups as well, especially in the Kargil region). Indeed, it is often called 'Little Tibet'. Due to the high altitude and mountainous terrain, the population is sparse. The capital town is Leh. Zanskar, in the south of Ladakh, is a distinctive subregion. The Aksai Chin region, a high and unpopulated plateau, has been under Chinese control since the 1962 Sino-Indian war.

To the north of the valley are extensive areas of uninhabited high mountains, including the Karakoram range, but with some areas of settlement in the valleys, for example Gilgit, Hunza and the Baltistan region. Two of the world's highest mountains, Nanga Parbat and K2, are located here, and the river Indus in its tumultuous mountain phase cuts through the whole vast region. Today these areas are mostly under the control of Pakistan, which has formed them into its federally administered Northern Areas. Since independence, Pakistan and China have constructed the Karakoram Highway along the Indus valley and through the high mountains, turning an ancient trade route into a motorable road. The construction of the road is one of the world's great civil engineering feats, although at the cost of many lives. The nature of the terrain is matched by a great cultural diversity.

Also under Pakistani control, but with an ambiguous legal status, is what is called by Pakistan 'Azad (Free) Kashmir' or sometimes 'Azad Jammu and Kashmir', and by India 'Pakistan-occupied Kashmir'. While the region is primarily Muslim, its language is closer to Punjabi than to Kashmiri. It includes territory drawn from both the Jammu and the Kashmir portions of the pre-1947 state. Since 1947, a major hydroelectric project, the Mangla dam, has been constructed in the region. Compared to the rest of the state there has been a substantial amount of migration to other parts of the world, especially Britain. The capital is Muzaffarabad.

People have lived in the regions described above since the earliest times. While the population is made up of different elements, the dominant group in most of the area is of Indo-Iranian origin, although Ladakh was settled from Tibet to the east. Kashmir has a unique historical document, Kalhana's *Rajatarangini*, a chronicle written in the 12th century CE. Even so, the early history of the region has to be mainly reconstructed from archaeological evidence and from knowledge of developments elsewhere. Buddhism made a major impact during the 3rd century BCE, during the reign of the emperor Ashoka and for some time thereafter; the first masterpieces of stone and bronze sculpture come from this period. Thereafter, the valley reverted to Hinduism, as did the rest of North India, and made a distinctive contribution to Hindu thought through the monist Shaivite philosophy, also known as the *Trika* system of thought. Compared to the *Advaita Vedanta* school of thought, Kashmiri Shaivism gives more weight to the actual world of the senses, and also recognizes tantric practices as a way to enlightenment. Abhinavagupta, a philosopher who lived in the second half of the 10th century CE, is a key figure in Kashmiri Shaivism. Kalhana tells us of major political figures, for example King Lalitaditya of the Karkota dynasty in the 8th century, who not only ruled wisely but also built one of the great temples of the region, the Martand temple. In the next century, Avantivarman, founder of the Utpala dynasty, was of a similar stature. Ladakh was initially under Tibetan control, but in 950 CE, an independent kingdom was established which survived under different dynasties until the early 19th century.

Islam came to Kashmir in the 13th and 14th centuries, and in 1320 the ruler of Kashmir at the time was converted. Over the years, many people followed suit. As elsewhere in India, Sufi saints such as Shah Hamadan and Nuruddin Rishi were important in this process. The 14th-century poetess, Lal Ded, who was born into a Hindu family but whose mystical poetry shows strong Sufi influences, indicates the high level of mutual respect and interaction between religious traditions in the region. This cultural fusion has been labelled *Kashmiriyat*, a word used to describe a distinct Kashmiri identity that transcends religious or community boundaries.

In 1586, the valley came under the control of the Mughal emperors, who were perhaps the first to use it as a refuge from the heat and dust of the plains. The emperor Akbar made three visits, and his son Jahangir, daughter-in-law Nur Jehan and grandson Shah Jehan were responsible for the world-famous Shalimar gardens near Srinagar. With the decline of the Mughal Empire in the 18th century, the region was affected by political upheavals elsewhere, especially in the Punjab. After a period of Afghan rule, in 1819 the state was brought into the Sikh Empire constructed by Ranjit Singh. During Ranjit Singh's long rule, one of his subordinate allies, Gulab Singh, who had begun his career as a local ruler of a state based on Jammu, first of all consolidated his position there and then extended his rule through an audacious campaign in Ladakh. Maharaja Gulab Singh switched sides during the struggles that followed Ranjit Singh's death in 1839 and, through his support of the British East India Company during the so-called first Sikh War, was not only confirmed as the ruler of Jammu and Ladakh but, by the Treaty of Amritsar in 1846, also purchased Kashmir for seven-and-a-half million rupees. During the remainder of the century, the Kashmir state attempted to exert its control over the small states to the north and west, notably Gilgit. Control of these states was, however, shared with the British, who were concerned about the general security of their Indian Empire, and in 1889 the Gilgit Agency was established (an earlier but short-lived experiment had been made between 1877 and 1881).

During the period from 1846 to the early 20th century, Kashmir's status as a 'princely state' within Britain's Indian Empire meant that it remained partly isolated from political developments elsewhere in South Asia. Successive Maharajas had a strained relationship with the British, whose overriding power was exercised through the Resident, as for example in 1889 when Maharaja Pratap Singh was divested of all effective power. However, in lesser matters the rulers were allowed a free hand. While a basic structure of government institutions was established, there was no attempt to recognize popular demands or to allow adequate representation of the Muslim majority population in the state bureaucracy. During the long period of colonial rule, the state became a favoured holiday retreat for British officials. Denied the right to own land, they used houseboats on the Dal Lake, next to Srinagar. In 1935, the British obtained a sixty-year lease on the area of the Gilgit Agency.

Kashmir's modern political history began in 1931, with the first major movement of political protest against the rule of the Maharajas. This brought to the fore a young Muslim leader, Sheikh Mohammad Abdullah. Initially identified with the Muslim Conference, he transformed the party into the National Conference in 1939 and gave it an increasingly secular and socialist orientation, thus bringing it closer to the Indian National Congress in British India, and Abdullah personally closer to Jawaharlal Nehru, whom he met for the first time in 1938. Although the Nehru family had lived outside the region since the 18th century, it had come originally from Kashmir and maintained its Pandit identity.

As the Second World War came to an end, it was clear that the new Labour Government really did intend to transfer power to Indian hands. Hectic political negotiations took place between the Congress, Mohammad Ali Jinnah's Muslim League and the British, represented at the end by Lord Mountbatten. Against a backdrop of increasing communal violence between Hindus and Muslims, especially in the Punjab, these three groups eventually produced a plan to partition India into Hindu and Muslim majority areas.

The fate of the princely states had, however, been given only limited attention, and nowhere was this more evident than in those cases where the religious affiliations of the ruler and his subjects differed. Jammu and Kashmir was not only the second biggest such state but its territory abutted both India and Pakistan. Although Maharaja Hari Singh had introduced a limited degree of constitutional reform in response to the 1931 agitation, there was little chance that it would satisfy the National Conference, which in 1946 launched a Quit Kashmir campaign, demanding that the Maharaja leave the state. Sheikh Abdullah was put on trial and sent to jail.

The mechanism provided for the princely states in the partition scheme that eventually took shape in the Indian Independence Act of July 1947 was that each ruler would have the right to decide the destiny of his state, whether this was to be accession to India or to Pakistan, or, at least theoretically, independence. There had, however, been no elections or other means to test popular Kashmiri opinion, and as independence approached in August 1947, the future of Kashmir was entirely unclear. Maharaja Hari Singh vacillated, while politicians in British India seem to have woken up very late to the situation. Sheikh Abdullah appears to have favoured some form of association with India. The rival Muslim Conference, however, preferred the Pakistan option.

On August 15th, 1947, the day when British rule ended, the state of Jammu and Kashmir was one of the few still not to have agreed to accede to one or other of the two new dominions of India and Pakistan. Thereafter, events moved rapidly and were soon beyond the control of any one group or individual. Much is uncertain or highly disputed. In August, there was a revolt against the Maharaja's rule in the Poonch area. In October, a large group of armed tribesmen from the North-West Frontier Province (by now part of Pakistan) entered the territory of the state and began to move towards Srinagar, terrorizing the population as they went. Faced with the imminent loss of his capital, Hari Singh eventually agreed to sign an instrument of accession to India. At the same time, the Indian government sent troops who arrived at Srinagar just in time to repel the invaders, themselves within a few miles of the town. In a separate development, the Gilgit area was taken over by Pakistan. Even this bald account, however, is problematic. The 'tribal invaders' seem to have been organized by regular officers from the Pakistan army, for example. A British historian, Alastair Lamb, has also claimed recently that the despatch of troops by India preceded rather than followed the signing of the instrument of accession. This analysis, which appears to undermine the legal basis of the Indian claim to the state, has been vigorously rebutted by Indian writers, for example Prem Shankar Jha.

The arrival of Indian troops led eventually to open hostilities with the Pakistan army, and during 1948 there were significant casualties on both sides. On the ground, India ended up controlling most of the Jammu region, the Kashmir Valley and Ladakh, while Pakistan was left controlling a western slice of Jammu and Kashmir and the vast and mountainous Northern Territories. Efforts by the newly formed United Nations produced both a cease-fire and a commitment that when both sides had withdrawn, a plebiscite would be held to determine to which country Kashmir would go. At the time of Maharaja Hari Singh's accession to India, Nehru had also referred to the need for a plebiscite to ascertain popular opinion. The two sides, however, could not agree on the terms on which the plebiscite could be held, despite the efforts of several UN-appointed mediators in the period up to 1953 (and occasionally thereafter). In 1954, India withdrew from any further discussions on the grounds that by obtaining arms from the United States, Pakistan had shown bad faith.

Nehru had initially placed great hope in Sheikh Abdullah, who became the first popular leader of the state, but by 1953 this had worn thin, as Abdullah showed signs of wanting to maintain too autonomous a position within the Indian Union (a position that appeared to be guaranteed by the special provisions made for the state under article 370 of the Indian constitution and confirmed by what came to be known as the Delhi Agreement of 1952 between Abdullah and Nehru). In 1953, he was arrested on the grounds that he was, in fact, working towards independence, and spent much of the period until 1968 in jail. Jammu and Kashmir was brought more firmly into the Indian political and constitutional framework, although article 370 remained in force. In 1957, a new state constitution was implemented which firmly asserted the state's membership of the Indian Union. Pliant political leaders were found to cooperate with Delhi, notably Abdullah's erstwhile colleague, Bakshi Ghulam Mohammed, while substantial subsidies supported the Kashmir economy. Indian strategy during this period was to encourage a gradual acceptance of their position as an integral part of India by the Muslim majority. Jammu and Kashmir was, in fact, the only Muslim-majority state within the Indian Union. Tensions continued, however, both between Kashmir and the rest of India, and between the inhabitants of the valley and those of Jammu, who felt excluded from political power. The mid-1960s were a time of particular turbulence.

Pakistan, meanwhile, continued to feel deeply wounded by what it saw as India's deceitful approach to the question, and never ceased to look for opportunities to keep the issue alive internationally. It maintained the position that the part of the state that had fallen to it in 1948 was still part of a single unit, whose final destination had still to be resolved. It therefore called it 'Azad Kashmir' (officially 'Azad Jammu and Kashmir'), and created a separate constitutional framework for it on that basis, with a president, prime minister and Supreme Court; Azad Kashmir has never received international recognition and for most purposes functions under the close supervision of the government in Islamabad. Pakistan did, however, separate out the former Gilgit Agency and merge it with Baltistan to form the 'Northern Areas', on the grounds that Gilgit had been leased to the British until the eve of independence, and had therefore come to Pakistan by right. In 1965, taking advantage of what was seen as a period of political and military weakness in India, Pakistan attempted a complex operation to coordinate an intervention by the army with an internal uprising to seize Kashmir. The moves failed and, following widespread fighting between the two countries in September, a cease-fire was again brokered by the United Nations. Talks were subsequently held under the auspices of the Soviet Union at Tashkent, which effectively left the status quo unchanged.

In 1971, India and Pakistan again went to war, this time over the position of East Pakistan, now Bangladesh. Although there was only a little fighting in the Kashmir area, the agreement that followed the Indian victory, the Simla (or Shimla) agreement of July 1972, included important clauses relating to the state. The cease-fire line was redesignated the line of control, while it was agreed that all outstanding issues should be resolved bilaterally, in Indian eyes at least thus eliminating any residual United Nations involvement. There have also been claims subsequently that there was a secret understanding between Mrs Gandhi and Mr Bhutto, the respective leaders of India and Pakistan, that the line of control should become the international border in due course. In 1972, Sheikh Abdullah was allowed to return to Kashmir; in 1974, negotiations led to an agreement with Mrs Gandhi that came into effect early the following year. This committed Abdullah to recognizing Kashmir's status within India and thus to renouncing efforts to obtain full autonomy. In return, it was agreed that article 370 would remain in force and, with the support of the Congress, Abdullah was reinstated as the state's Chief Minister, a position he held until his death in 1982.

Sheikh Abdullah was succeeded as Chief Minister by his son, Dr Farooq Abdullah, who attempted to continue the difficult task of exercising power in Srinagar while supporting the government in Delhi. However, his political standing in no way matched his father's, and he had difficulty in coping with the increasingly centralized Indian polity, symbolized by the actions of first Mrs Gandhi and then, after her assassination in October 1984, her son Rajiv Gandhi. Dismissed under controversial circumstances by Governor Jagmohan in July 1984, Farooq Abdullah returned to power in 1986 in alliance with the Congress party of Rajiv Gandhi, but the subsequent elections in 1987 were marred by widespread allegations of electoral fraud.

Among the Muslim population as a whole, a number of different trends had emerged by the 1980s. On the one hand, a number of political leaders hankered after the idea of a plebiscite as originally envisaged, and were willing to think of direct links with Pakistan. The Awami Action Committee, led by the leading Muslim cleric of the valley, took this line. On the other hand, a newer generation were beginning to recast the question in terms of a general right of ethnic groups to self-determination and a national identity. The Jammu and Kashmir Liberation Front (JKLF), founded in 1965, was particularly prominent in this respect, but there were other groups as well. By contrast, the majority of the Hindu population were fearful for their future under any arrangements that denied them the full protection of New Delhi. Another group anxious about the future were the Buddhists of Ladakh.

Matters began to come to a head during 1988 and at the end of 1989 a full-scale insurrection began. Estimates vary but at a minimum, 25,000 people died in the following decade, and the figure may be much higher. Victims have come from all sections and communities, civilians, security forces and militants alike. A large proportion of the Pandit community fled the valley in fear of their lives, although many believe that the initial exodus was an exaggerated response. Interpretations of the conflict reflect the underlying diametrically opposed perspectives on Kashmir. For most Indians, the problem is very largely of Pakistan's creation, with only a minority of misguided Kashmiris participating. Much is made of the availability of 'mercenaries' and weapons following the end of the Afghan war at the end of the 1980s, especially after the main national insurgents, the JKLF, called a cease-fire in 1994. Islamic fundamentalism is also blamed for the intransigence of the rebels, while the West is blamed for applying a double standard when it condemns alleged human rights abuses without recognizing the real problem in the region, i.e. Pakistan-sponsored subversion. Pakistan sees the matter straightforwardly as the unfinished business of partition in 1947, and that without a just solution to the rightful demands of the Kashmiri people, violence remains inevitable. The assumption that a Muslim-majority area must want to be part of Pakistan is rarely subject to scrutiny. Many Muslim Kashmiris reject the assertion of Indian sovereignty over their territory, but have become increasingly sceptical about their prospects were they to join Pakistan.

Since 1989, the uprising has, in fact, passed through several phases. Once the initial confrontations had been met by a massive movement into the state of Indian security forces, a guerrilla war developed. A number of individuals were assassinated, and on two occasions militants occupied major Muslim holy places. On the second occasion, in 1995, the shrine of Charar-i-Sharif was destroyed in the ensuing battle. An increasing number of militants from Pakistan and further afield have become involved. From time to time there have been planned attacks on members of the Hindu minority. The Indian response throughout has been to combine military repression, often with scant regard for the niceties of legal process, with attempts to identify groups that would collaborate in an internal solution based on the constitutional status quo. On the other side, a broad alliance of opposition groups, the

Hurriyat Conference, emerged, many of them with links to militant groups. In 1994, the JKLF declared a cease-fire, although other groups continued their armed campaigns. In 1996, it was eventually possible to hold elections, first in May to the Indian Parliament and then in September to the state assembly. Although the turnout was less than fifty per cent, with a boycott by the Hurriyat Conference, and there were claims of coerced voting, the elections opened the way for the return to power of Farooq Abdullah (who had resigned from office at the beginning of the insurgency). To many Kashmiris there seemed at least the possibility of political movement.

Since 1996, however, Farooq Abdullah has made little real headway in achieving an 'internal solution' to the state's problems. Although the level of overt violence has decreased as a result of the security forces' actions, the alienation of the majority of the population in the valley is evident. The recommendations of two committees set up to consider respectively the state's relations with Delhi and the internal relations between the component parts of the state (to assuage fears in Jammu and Ladakh about Kashmiri domination) have not been implemented. While Farooq Abdullah has been able to achieve an understanding with the right-wing Bharatiya Janata Party (BJP) government of Atal Behari Vajpayee, in power since 1998, this has mainly served to maintain his own position and the status quo rather than to move forward. In 1999, there was a serious outbreak of fighting between Indian and Pakistani forces along the line of control in the vicinity of the town of Kargil. Only after intervention from the United States did Pakistan agree to withdraw its forces. Inevitably, world opinion was concerned about the risk of escalation of the conflict between two countries that, the previous year, had conducted nuclear tests. Tensions were again raised by a hijack of an Indian Airlines plane in December 1999 by a group demanding the release of a Pakistani militant leader, and during President Clinton's visit to South Asia in March 2000, militants massacred thirty-five members of Kashmir's small Sikh minority.

Many different proposals have been put forward over the years for the solution of the Kashmir dispute. The official positions of India and Pakistan regard the state as a single entity; many Kashmiris hold to the same view, but often with the proviso that this should open up the third option of independence or full autonomy, perhaps through some form of confederal arrangement. Ideas have been discussed at various times of an Indo-Pakistan condominium over the state, combined with a high degree of local autonomy. Other proposals are based on some sort of partition of the state. In one version, deriving from a plan put forward in 1950 by Sir Owen Dixon, one of the UN mediators, this would leave Jammu and Ladakh with India, and the present Pakistan-held parts with Pakistan, with the valley being allowed to choose through the means of a plebiscite (plebiscites in the other regions would be foregone conclusions). A further approach argues that the realities of the Indo-Pakistan relationship are such that no significant territorial shift can be expected, and that therefore the present de facto border, the line of control, should at some point be converted into a recognized international border (proponents of this view often look to the Simla agreement as the beginnings of such a process). For this to happen, and for it to be acceptable to the main protagonists, substantial political change would have to take place both internally and between India and Pakistan.

The Region and Its People

1 Ladakh: the trans-Himalayan kingdom.
Ramesh Bedi. Delhi: Roli Books International, 1981. 192p.
The book essentially consists of a collection of high-quality colour photographs taken by Rajesh Bedi. The pictures are grouped by subject (daily life, folklore, etc.), and each group has a brief introduction by Ramesh Bedi.

2 Kashmiri Pandits: a cultural heritage.
Edited by S. Bhatt. Delhi: Lancers Books, 1995. 631p. bibliog.
The editor has organized a team of some sixty contributors, almost all of them members of the Pandit community, who write about Kashmiri religion, language and culture, with special reference to the Pandit community, and about the Pandits themselves, past and present. The tone is celebratory.

3 Ladák, physical, statistical and historical; with notices of the surrounding countries.
Alexander Cunningham. London: W. H. Allen, 1854. 485p.
Based on two visits to Ladakh in 1846 and 1847, this is the earliest systematic work on the region by a European. Chapters are devoted to various aspects of its physical geography, its history, people and religion. Cunningham was an assiduous scholar and his work was mined for information by later writers.

4 Kashmiri cooking.
Krishna Prasad Dar. Ghaziabad, India: Vikas, 1977. 160p.
This is a straightforward collection of recipes with vegetarian and non-vegetarian sections put together by a multi-talented member of the Kashmiri Pandit community (among other things he printed some of the writings of his fellow-Kashmiri, Jawaharlal Nehru). Like many others, his family had moved from Kashmir to North India but preserved the community's culinary traditions.

1

5 An introduction to South Asia.
B. H. Farmer.   London, New York: Routledge, 1993. 2nd ed. 197p.
maps.

A brief and businesslike general introduction to the subcontinent. Farmer discusses
the physical environment, history, political and economic development, and
international relations of the region. Jammu and Kashmir are referred to at various
points, and there is specific coverage of the Kashmir dispute between India and
Pakistan.

6 A cultural history of Kashmir and Kishtawar.
F. M. Hassnain.   Delhi: Rima Publishing House, 1992. 186p.
bibliog.

This is a rather general account that covers not only cultural history in the narrow sense
but also geographical and zoological topics. The greater part of the book is devoted to the
history of the small kingdom of Kishtawar, the part of Kashmir on the upper stretch of the
Chenab River, and covers the period up to 1821, when the region was absorbed into
Jammu.

7 Heritage of Kashmir.
Edited by F. M. Hassnain.   Srinagar, India: Gulshan Publishers, 1980.
239p. bibliog.

A highly miscellaneous collection of papers of somewhat uneven quality, originally given
at a seminar in 1976. Subjects range from ancient history and Islam in Kashmir to
veterinary medicine in the region. A concluding chapter by the editor lauds the state's
composite culture.

8 Search for a magic carpet.
Frances Hawker, Bruce Campbell.   London: Evans Brothers; Milton,
Queensland: Jacaranda Wiley, 1981. 28p.

This is a book for young children that uses the story of two Kashmiri children's search for
a magic carpet to introduce basic information about Kashmiri life. The text is written in
simple language and there are many colour photographs of domestic life. A very similar
book, focused on a boy from a family of houseboat owners, is *A week in Lateef's world:
India* by Charlotte Zolotow (London: Crowell-Collier Press, 1970), although it uses
black-and-white rather than colour photographs.

9 Ladakh: the land and the people.
Prem Singh Jina.   Delhi: Indus Publishing Company, 1996. 288p.
maps. bibliog.

A general introduction to the region, compiled from secondary sources, covering aspects
ranging from its physical geography and its trade and economy to social and religious
customs.

10 Travels in Kashmir: a popular history of its people, places and crafts.
Brigid Keenan.   Oxford: Oxford University Press, 1990. 226p. maps. bibliog.

This book is an excellent introduction to Kashmir for the visitor and general reader. Brigid Keenan writes as a sympathetic visitor anxious to understand the area's history and its cultural traditions. Equal space is devoted to its early history, especially the Mughal period, its role as a resort for the Raj, and its arts and crafts, shawl-weaving and papier-mâché work in particular. The author is skilled at the illuminating anecdote or story, for example the mid-19th-century comedy of Mrs Hervey and Captain H. This book would make a fine companion for the first-time visitor to the valley. It was written, of course, before the beginning of the present troubles in the late 1980s, although it was not published until 1990.

11 Proceedings of the Csoma de Kőrös Memorial Symposium held at Mátrafüred, Hungary 24-30 September 1976.
Edited by Louis Ligeti.   Budapest: Akademiai Kiado, 1978. 586p.

Koros was a 19th-century Hungarian savant who, in the 1820s, was one of the first Europeans to visit Ladakh (he later explored Tibet itself). Apart from a paper devoted to Koros' stay in Ladakh, the present volume is mostly devoted to linguistic and religious topics concerned with Tibet as a whole, although there are some references to Ladakh.

12 Beyond the Pir Panjal: life and missionary enterprise in Kashmir.
Ernest F. Neve.   London: Church Missionary Society, 1915. 178p.

A standard missionary memoir written to call others to Kashmir in pursuit of converts and opportunities for service in the medical and educational fields. It includes detailed descriptions both of Srinagar at the beginning of the 20th century and of the daily activities of the mission hospitals and schools. C. E. Tyndale-Biscoe's *Kashmir in sunlight and shade* (London: Seeley Service, 1925) is written along similar lines.

13 Ancient futures: learning from Ladakh.
Helena Norberg-Hodge.   San Francisco: Sierra Club, 1991; London: Rider, 1992. 204p. map. bibliog.

First published in the US in 1991, this book is dedicated to the proposition that modern societies have much to learn from more self-reliant societies such as Ladakh. The author has lived for part of each year in Ladakh for a long time, and the book includes a great deal of detailed information about the culture of Ladakh. There is a preface by the Dalai Lama, and the author sees its Tibetan Buddhist heritage as one of the strengths of Ladakhi culture. She is, however, acutely conscious of the way that the local culture is being eroded by the pressures of foreign tourism. The author was instrumental in establishing the Ladakh Project (now known as the International Society for Ecology and Culture) to support the Ladakhi way of life, and she describes its work, which has been influenced by the writings of the founder of the appropriate technology movement, E. F. Schumacher, in the last chapter.

14 Recent research on Ladakh.
Edited by Henry Osmaston et al. Various imprints, 1995- .

Every year or two, a wide range of scholars from Ladakh and abroad have come together to attend an international conference, and each conference has resulted in a publication. The first volumes in the series were produced under different titles: *Recent research on Ladakh: history, culture, sociology, ecology*, edited by Detlef Kantowsky & Reinhard Sander (Munich: Weltforum Verlag, 1983); *Ladakh, Himalaya Occidental: ethnologie, ecologie*, edited by Claude Dentaletche (Paris: Centre Pyrenéen de Biologie et Anthropologie des Montagnes, 1985); *Wissenschaftsgeschichte und gegenwärtige Forschungen in nordwest-Indien*, edited by Lydia Icke-Schwalbe & Gudrun Meier (Dresden, Germany: Staatliches Museum fur Völkerkunde, 1990); *Himalayan Buddhist villages: environment, resources, society and religious life in Zangskar, Ladakh*, edited by John H. Crook & Henry Osmaston (Bristol, England: University of Bristol Press, 1993). Since the fourth conference, volumes have been produced under a common title, with Henry Osmaston providing editorial continuity. The most recent volume is number 6, published in 1997 (Delhi: Motilal Banarsidass). Most items are in English, but there are some in French, German and Ladakhi (often with an English version as well). They cover religious, historical and anthropological topics, as well as some related to economic and social development. Another collection of papers on the region is *Recent researches on the Himalaya*, edited by Prem Singh Jina (Delhi: Indus, 1997).

15 Zanskar: a Himalayan kingdom.
Jacques Poget. London: Thames & Hudson, 1989. unpaginated. map.

Originally published in French (Paris: Editions Nathan, 1988), the book contains a short introduction evoking the heritage of Zanskar (the southern part of Ladakh) and the role within it of Tibetan culture. There then follow 102 colour plates designed to bring out the essence of the people and the immensity of the landscape. The photographs are often carefully constructed to heighten the artistic impact.

16 Ladakh: crossroads of high Asia.
Janet Rizvi. Delhi, Oxford: Oxford University Press, 1996. 2nd ed. 290p. map. bibliog.

First published in 1983, this enlarged version brings together a remarkable range of information and research on the history, culture and present condition of Ladakh, including much that has been published only recently. The style is popular but always true to the material. The book is well illustrated with black-and-white and colour photographs.

17 The Cambridge encyclopedia of India, Pakistan, Sri Lanka, Nepal, Bhutan and the Maldives.
Edited by Francis Robinson. Cambridge, England: Cambridge University Press, 1989. 520p. maps. bibliog.

An up-to-date survey of the whole subcontinent, including Kashmir and Ladakh, produced by numerous scholars from the region and from outside. Although termed an encyclopaedia, it is arranged by subject rather than alphabetically, with short articles covering aspects of history, economics, society and culture. It is attractively designed and illustrated.

18   Encyclopaedia of Kashmir.
Edited by Suresh K. Sharma, S. R. Bakshi.   Delhi: Anmol Publications, 1995. 10 vols.

This large work is perhaps not so much an encyclopaedia as a digest of material for the study of Kashmir. It consists almost entirely of extracts from previously published work. Depending on the subject of the volume, this could be in the form of historical articles, texts of speeches, correspondence between political leaders or UN resolutions. The original location is indicated for some but not all the items. The themes of the volumes are respectively: ancient and medieval Kashmir; Kashmir art, architecture and tourism; Kashmir during British rule; Modern Kashmir; Kashmir – the constitutional status; Nehru and Kashmir; Sheikh Abdullah and Kashmir; Kashmir and the United Nations; Kashmir society and culture; Economic life of Kashmir.

19   Kashmir: garden of the Himalayas.
Raghubir Singh.   London: Thames & Hudson, 1983. 32p. map.

One of India's best-known photographers, Raghubir Singh uses his text and the eighty accompanying (unpaginated) colour photographs to extol the cultural and social harmony of Kashmir society. The ravishingly beautiful pictures are of people at work and relaxing, as well as of scenery and gardens. The book is prefaced by an extended extract from Jawaharlal Nehru's autobiography, in which he describes his emotional link to the land his forbears left in the early 18th century.

20   Story of Kashmir.
Prithvi Nath Tikoo.   Delhi: Light and Life Publishers, 1979. 287p. bibliog.

A popular account of Kashmir written by a member of the Pandit community, and perhaps reflecting that group's view of the state's history.

21   The heritage of Kashmir.
Vijaya R. Trivedi.   Delhi: Mohit Publications, 1996. 351p. bibliog.

Arranged in encyclopaedia format, this work includes entries for a wide variety of subjects ranging from topography, wildlife and cookery to biographical sketches. Although the organization is weak, especially in the absence of an index, there are some interesting items.

22   Kashmir.
Francis Younghusband, illustrated by E. Molyneux.   London: A. & C. Black, 1909. 283p. map.

Younghusband was one of the most important of the late 19th-century British officials in India, and was frequently involved with imperial machinations in Tibet and Central Asia. He was British Resident (i.e. the representative of British authority) in Kashmir in the first years of the 20th century. He was at the same time deeply interested in Buddhism. The book combines descriptions of tourist sites with more gazetteer-like chapters on manufactures, agriculture, system of administration, etc. and is illustrated with reproductions of water colours by E. Molyneux depicting scenes on the Dal lake and in the mountains. The book was reprinted in 1970, complete with illustrations (Delhi: Sagar Publications). Younghusband has been the subject of several biographies, most recently by Patrick French (*Younghusband: the last great imperial adventurer*, London: HarperCollins, 1994).

Geography

General

23 Historical geography of Kashmir.
S. Maqbul Ahmad, Raja Bano.   Delhi: Ariana Publishing House,
1984. 230p. bibliog.
This work is, in fact, a compilation of topographical and geographical material on
Kashmir drawn from Arabic and Persian sources. The writers cited date from 800 CE to
1900 CE. The authors refer to Aurel Stein's memoir on the ancient geography of Kashmir
(included in his translation of the *Rajatarangini* – see entry no. 124), and seek to provide
a complementary account for the medieval period.

**24 The northern barrier of India. A popular account of the Jummoo
and Kashmir territories.**
Frederic Drew.   London: Edward Stanford, 1877. 336p. maps.
Drew worked for the Maharaja and travelled extensively during the course of this work,
and this book is essentially a descriptive geography of the state, including all the
territories under the Maharaja's sway. There is a great deal of rather dry ethnographic and
historical information, combined with accounts of the rules of polo as played in Gilgit.
Drew is not afraid to comment unselfconsciously on the hygienic habits of the inhabitants
or on the supposed racial characteristics of one group or another, which he illustrates with
photographs. The text (but not the maps and photographs) was reprinted in 1971 (Jammu,
India: Light and Life Publishers). Drew was also the author of a larger work along the
same lines, *The Jummoo and Kashmir territories: a geographical account* (London:
Edward Stanford, 1875).

25 Bibliography of the Himalayas.
R. K. Gupta.   Gurgaon, India: Indian Documentation Service, 1981.
375p.
The 4,772 unannotated entries are derived from a very wide range of specialist academic
and technical journals and cover physical and human aspects of the region's geography,

together with flora and fauna. There is no index and the work is divided purely thematically rather than by the five sub-regions identified in the introduction, one of which is the Kashmir area.

26 Roads and rivals: the political uses of access in the borderlands of Asia.
Mahnaz Z. Ispahani. Ithaca, New York; London: Cornell University Press, 1989. 286p. maps. bibliog.

An exercise in political geography which examines the importance of physical communication in the strategic decisions of policymakers in Pakistan and elsewhere. The fourth chapter looks at the routes that connect Pakistan with China through the Karakoram Mountains. In the 1970s, the track was converted into a motorable road. Part of this passes through the Northern Areas, and thus through territory claimed by India. India has often protested about the threat the road poses to its security interests. The author outlines the history of the construction of the road and discusses its strategic significance.

27 The Himalaya: aspects of change.
J. S. Lall, in association with A. D. Moddie. Delhi, Oxford: Oxford University Press, 1981. 481p. maps. bibliog.

Published on behalf of Delhi's well-known India International Centre, this volume contains a diverse set of papers by Indian and foreign authors on many aspects of Himalayan ecology, culture and society. Some of the papers are detailed studies, others quite general in scope. Several focus specifically on Ladakh.

28 A handbook of the Himalaya.
S. S. Negi. Delhi: Indus Publishing Company, 1990. 350p. maps. bibliog.

This is essentially a regional geography of the Himalayan mountains that places Jammu and Kashmir within its physical environment. Topics covered include geology, soils, river systems, environmental issues, flora and fauna, and social groups (although only patchily). In practice, the data relating to Jammu and Kashmir concerns only the Indian-controlled portions of the state.

29 The valley of Kashmir: a geographical interpretation. Vol. 1, The land.
Moonis Raza, Aijazuddin Ahmad, Ali Mohammad. Durham, North Carolina: Carolina Academic Press, 1978. 148p. maps. bibliog.

Based on a wide range of mostly government sources, this volume deals with the physical geography of the Kashmir valley, and covers climate, geomorphology, river systems, vegetation, soils and related topics. Although it was originally intended as part of a three-volume work, the other volumes were never published.

30   India and Pakistan: a general and regional geography.
O. H. K. Spate, A. T. A. Learmonth.   London: Methuen, 1967. 3rd
ed. 877p. maps. bibliog.

Although a little dated, this remains the most comprehensive and reliable geographical
survey of the Indian subcontinent. The authors are generous in their definition of the
geographical and discuss many aspects of historical and economic development. Kashmir
is given its own chapter, and there are references to the state in other sections as well. The
specifically regional chapters of the work were published separately in 1972 – see *India,
Pakistan and Ceylon: the regions*, by Spate, Learmonth and B. H. Farmer (London:
Methuen). Spate contributed a much briefer review of the subcontinent to *The changing
map of Asia: a political geography*, edited by W. Gordon East, O. H. K. Spate and Charles
Fisher (London: Methuen, 1971. 5th ed.).

31   South Asia: a systematic geographic bibliography.
B. L. Sukhwal.   Metuchen, New Jersey: Scarecrow Press, 1974.
827p.

A well-prepared but unannotated bibliography that lists 10,346 items arranged according
to all the standard geographical categories – economic, physical, human and political.
Unpublished US dissertations are included, as are numerous journal articles from South
Asia and abroad. There are, in fact, a substantial number of entries relating to Jammu and
Kashmir, but the usefulness of the volume is severely restricted by the absence of a
subject index to amplify the country-based table of contents.

Maps and gazetteers

32   A gazetteer of Kashmír.
Charles Ellison Bates.   Calcutta, India: Office of the Superintendent
of Government Printing, 1873. 560p. map.

Intended primarily for the use of military officers and government officials, this follows
the pattern of gazetteers compiled for other parts of India in the 19th century. The first
100 or so pages give general information on the state's history, economy and
administrative structures, while the rest of the volume is devoted to a minute description
of each town and village and of the routes which connect them. The volume was reprinted
in 1980 (Delhi: Light and Life Publishers).

**33   An atlas of the Mughal empire: political and economic maps with
detailed notes, bibliography and index.**
Irfan Habib.   Oxford, Delhi: Oxford University Press, 1982. 105p.
maps. bibliog.

This volume is primarily intended for the specialist historian but might be of some use to
others, although the black-and-white maps are not in themselves especially alluring. The
Mughal empire is divided into sixteen blocks, for each of which there are two maps at a
scale of 1:2,000,000 giving political and economic information respectively. Kashmir

forms one such block. The extensive notes give sources for place-name identification and other information contained on the maps, and provide discussions of the issues raised. As Habib, the leading present-day historian of the Mughals, states in his introduction, the period is remarkably rich in sources for the modern mapmaker, and an immense amount of information can be derived from the maps.

34 The imperial gazetteer of India: the Indian empire.
Oxford: Clarendon Press, 1907-09. 26 vols.

The first attempt to produce a comprehensive gazetteer of the Indian Empire was made in 1881, an enterprise which resulted in a work of a mere nine volumes. The 1907-09 version, produced at the height of the British Raj, was twenty-six volumes in length. Four served as general description, one was an index, one an atlas, and the remaining twenty contained alphabetically arranged notes on every place and region of any significance in the whole country. A modern publication which follows the same pattern and draws heavily on recently produced official district gazetteers is *The encyclopaedic district gazetteers of India*, edited by S. C. Bhatt (Delhi: Gyan Publishing House, 1997). Volume three includes 156 pages devoted to Jammu and Kashmir.

35 Indian subcontinent: India, Pakistan, Bangladesh, Sri Lanka.
Edinburgh: John Bartholomew, [n.d.]. (Bartholomew World Travel Map).

This widely available and frequently reprinted map covers the whole subcontinent at a scale of 1:4,000,000. The physical features, main communications network and urban centres are all clearly shown. The usual conventions are followed in depicting the borders of Jammu and Kashmir (i.e., no international border is shown, the original state boundaries are shown in the same thickness as Indian and Pakistani internal borders, and the line of control is shown as a dotted line). The cartography of the map is also used for the *Times atlas of the world* (London: Times Books, 1980. 6th ed.).

36 The valley of Kashmir.
Walter R. Lawrence.   London: Henry Frowde, 1895. 478p. map.

Lawrence was a senior official in Jammu and Kashmir, employed to deal with general questions of revenue. This volume, which deals only with Kashmir, provides a great deal of information on the area, covering flora and fauna, history, religious beliefs, and the economy. There are some photographic illustrations. Lawrence also prepared the Kashmir and Jammu section of the *Imperial gazetteer of India*, entitled *Kashmir and Jammu* (Calcutta: Superintendent of Government Printing, 1909).

37 Pakistan – an official handbook.
Islamabad: Directorate General of Films and Publications, Ministry of Information and Broadcasting, Government of Pakistan.

Published on a more or less annual basis, this essentially public relations-oriented publication includes two chapters in each issue on Azad Kashmir and the Northern Areas respectively. Given that these areas are excluded from most official Pakistani sources, e.g. census publications, these volumes provide some basic data.

38   A historical atlas of South Asia.
Edited by Joseph E. Schwartzberg.   New York, Oxford: Oxford
University Press, 1992. 2nd ed. 376p. maps. bibliog. (Association for
Asian Studies Reference Series, no. 2).

The product of many years of work by Schwartzberg and his colleagues, this atlas (first published in 1978 by Chicago University Press) quickly established itself as a uniquely valuable research tool. The numerous large and small maps are divided into fourteen sections covering historical periods from the prehistoric to the contemporary and political, economic and social developments. On Kashmir, there are maps that show not only the disputed boundaries but also distributions of population in terms of language and religion. Each section of maps has a paired chapter of text that provides background information and commentary. The bibliography is also particularly extensive and useful.

Flora and Fauna

39   Compact handbook of the birds of India and Pakistan.
Sálim Ali, S. Dillon Ripley, plates by John Henry Dick.   Delhi:
Oxford University Press, 1987. 2nd ed. 737p. maps. bibliog.

Ali and his American colleague Ripley are the universally acknowledged doyens of
modern ornithology in South Asia and, therefore, the Kashmir region. Their magnum
opus was the *Handbook of the birds of India and Pakistan*, published originally in ten
volumes from 1968 to 1975 (Bombay: Oxford University Press). A second edition is
gradually being issued. The *Compact handbook*, published originally in 1983, by using
small but legible print manages to get all the text into a single large volume. The second
edition incorporates the revised editions of the first four volumes. It also includes an
entirely new set of illustrations, some in colour and some in black and white. Closely
connected to the *Handbook* are Salim Ali, *The book of Indian birds* (Delhi: Oxford
University Press, 1979. 11th ed.), the best single-volume work for the amateur, and S.
Dillon Ripley, *A synopsis of the birds of India and Pakistan* (Bombay: Natural History
Society, 1982. 2nd ed.).

**40   Encyclopedia of Indian natural history: centenary publication of
the Bombay Natural History Society, 1883-1983.**
Edited by R. E. Hawkins, illustrations edited by Doris Norden, Bittu
Sahgal.   Delhi: Oxford University Press for the Bombay Natural
History Society, 1986. 620p. map.

This volume lists in alphabetical order several hundred species and categories of species
of all types of plant and animal life to be found in South Asia, including Jammu and
Kashmir. The entries are written by experts but intended to convey up-to-date, non-
technical information to a general readership. There are many well-reproduced drawings
and black-and-white photographs in the text, and forty plates of colour and black-and-
white illustrations.

41   Flowers of the Himalaya.
Oleg Polunin, Adam Stainton.   Oxford, England; New York: Oxford
University Press, 1984. 580p. maps. bibliog.

Intended as a field guide, this volume identifies all the common species that belong to the Himalayan flora. The fieldwork covered the Indian-held part of Kashmir only, although many of the plants described would also be found further west. Each of the 1,495 entries is given a full scientific description. There are 689 colour photographs and 316 line drawings. A concise edition, including all the illustrations but with abbreviated descriptions, was published in 1988. An earlier work devoted exclusively to Kashmir is by Ethelbert Blatter, *Beautiful flowers of Kashmir* (London: John Bale, Sons & Danielsson, 1927. 2 vols.).

42   Mountain monarchs: wild sheep and goats of the Himalaya.
George B. Schaller.   Chicago, London: University of Chicago Press,
1977. 425p. map. bibliog.

A scientific study based on over two years of research in Pakistan, mainly in the Northern Areas, on the ecology and behavioural patterns of the wild sheep and goats of the Himalaya. The author is particularly concerned with those species about which little has been written previously, for example the urial, wild goat and bharal. The work is well illustrated both with photographs and with tables of information on distribution, physical characteristics, etc. Schaller also wrote *Stones of silence: journeys in the Himalaya* (London: André Deutsch, 1980), which is based on the same research but takes a broader view of the environment of the regions in which he travelled. Meetings with George Schaller on a later visit to the area are reported in Galen Rowell's book (see entry no. 66).

Travellers' Accounts

43 Hermit kingdom: Ladakh.
H. P. S. Ahluwalia. Delhi: Himalayan Books, 1987. 170p. map.
bibliog.

This travel book includes extensive references to Ladakh's history and culture. Much of the book is devoted to the author's visit to the remote Nubra valley. There are many well-reproduced colour photographs.

44 Mountains of the Murgha Zerin: between the Hindu Khush and the Karakoram.
Elizabeth Balneaves. London: John Gifford, 1972. 239p. bibliog.

This is an account of an extended journey in the Northern Areas of Pakistan by a writer who had made a number of previous visits to the region. The latter part of the book covers her travels in Gilgit and Baltistan. The date of the journey is not mentioned but internal evidence dates it to the late 1960s. However, there is a somewhat old-fashioned feel to much of the writing.

45 Travels in the Mogul empire, A. D. 1657-1668.
Francois Bernier, translated by Archibald Constable, revised by Vincent A. Smith. London: Oxford University Press, 1934. 2nd ed. 497p.

Bernier was a French doctor who found his way to India in the 17th century and stayed for some years at the court of the Mughal emperor, Aurangzeb. He travelled to Kashmir in the train of Aurangzeb in 1665, and his letters to friends in France printed here contain very detailed accounts of Kashmir at that time. Extracts from his travels, including the Kashmir section, were reprinted as *Aurangzeb in Kashmir (Travels in the Mughal empire)*, edited by D. C. Sharma (Delhi: Rima Publishing House, 1988).

46   Hunza: lost kingdom of the Himalayas.

John Clark.   London: Hutchinson, 1957. 262p. map.

A personal account of nearly two years spent in Hunza at the beginning of the 1950s by an American scientist who set up a craft school there as his individual contribution to the fight against communism. The book details his battles with local bureaucrats and others who were suspicious of what he was doing, as well as his day-to-day work with his students and his pleasure in the life of the area.

47   A viceroy's India: leaves from Lord Curzon's note-book.

Curzon, Marquess of Kedleston, edited by Peter King.   London: Sidgwick & Jackson, 1984. 192p. map.

This volume brings together selections from Lord Curzon's two volumes of essays written while he was viceroy of India from 1899 to 1905, including several pieces on his travels in Kashmir and further north into Gilgit and beyond. The pieces are notable for Curzon's effortlessly imperial style as much as for the actual content.

48   A journey from Bengal to England through the northern part of India, Kashmire, Afghanistan, and Persia and into Russia by the Caspian Sea.

George Forster.   London: R. Faulder & Son, 1808. 2nd ed. 2 vols.

In 1783, Forster, an East India Company official, travelled overland from India to England. His book, originally published in Calcutta in 1790, is in the form of a daily diary with observations on what he saw as he went along. There are extensive passages on Kashmir at a time before it had been conquered by the Sikhs. There are 1990 and 1997 reprints (Delhi: Munshi Manoharlal).

49   This is Kashmir.

Pearce Gervis.   London: Cassell, 1954. 330p. map.

This book is a run-of-the-mill travelogue from the early 1950s, but it has some interest as a transitional piece between the Raj style of writing and present-day travel guides.

50   Nanga Parbat.

Karl M. Herrligkoffer.   London: Elek Books, 1954. 254p. bibliog.

Nanga Parbat is one of the highest peaks of the Himalaya, located in the Karakoram Mountains along with K2. Both peaks have attracted many expeditions over the last century. Herrligkoffer's book, originally in German, gives an account of the expedition he led in 1953 which first conquered the peak. Hermann Buhl was the climber to reach the summit. Unlike some other mountaineering stories, it pays due tribute to the many earlier expeditions from 1895 onwards.

51   Travels in Kashmir and the Panjab.

Charles [Carl von] Hügel.   London: John Petheram, 1845. 423p. map.

This English work was extracted and translated by T. B. Jervis from a larger work by Baron von Hügel, a German traveller who visited Kashmir in the 1830s, where he met Vigne (see entry no. 70). Hügel was a close observer of the social and political situation in the region. There are Pakistani (Lahore: Qausain, 1976) and Indian (Patiala: Government of the Punjab, 1970) reprints. Other sections of Hügel's original which deal with the detail of economic conditions have been translated and edited by D. C. Sharma as *Kashmir under Maharaja Ranjit Singh: its artistic products, taxation system, imports and exports, and trade* (Delhi: Atlantic Publishers, c.1984).

52   Letters from India; describing a journey in the British dominions of India, Tibet, Lahore, and Cashmere during the years 1828, 1829, 1830, 1831 undertaken by orders of the French government.
Victor Jacquemont, introduction by John Rosselli.   Karachi, Pakistan: Oxford University Press, 1979. 2 vols. map. (Oxford in Asia Historical Reprints).

First published in English in 1834, this work was widely read in the 19th century both in France and in Britain. Its author went to India on a scientific expedition to collect botanical specimens but soon made contacts among British officials and Indian rulers. Although Jacquemont shared most of the European prejudices of his time, his letters to family and friends are marked, in the words of Rosselli's useful introduction to the modern edition, by a 'morning freshness' of perception. During his travels he made extensive visits to both Punjab and Kashmir, although less so to those parts that are now in Pakistan or Azad Kashmir.

53   Famous western explorers to Ladakh.
Prem Singh Jina.   Delhi: Indus Publishing Company, c. 1995. 152p. bibliog.

This book contains a pot-pourri of material, drawn from a wide range of travellers' accounts of the region from the 17th century to the present day.

54   Travels in South Asia: a selected and annotated bibliography of guide-books and travel-books on South Asia.
Edited by H. K. Kaul.   Delhi: Arnold-Heinemann, 1979. 215p.

Contains 1,016 well-annotated entries, based on the holdings of a number of libraries in Delhi. Many of the items, both in the travel and the guidebook sections, relate to the Kashmir region. The bibliography is particularly strong on the pre-1947 period.

55   Where men and mountains meet: the explorers of the western Himalayas 1820-75.
John Keay.   Karachi, Pakistan: Oxford University Press, 1993. 277p. maps. bibliog.

First published in 1977 (London: John Murray), this is perhaps the most accessible account of the various European traders, spies and eccentrics who first visited the western Himalayan region. Kashmir naturally forms a major focus of the work, and Keay writes racy accounts of figures such as Moorcroft (see entry no. 62), Vigne (see entry no. 70), and Jacquemont (see entry no. 52). Keay also published a sequel, *The Gilgit game: the explorers of the western Himalayas 1865-95* (London: John Murray, 1979), which concentrates on the period when exploration was more closely linked to the manoeuvres of the British and Russian empires along their common frontier, and covers figures such as G. W. Leitner (see entry no. 292), the Durand brothers (see entry no. 135) and Francis Younghusband (see entry no. 22).

56 Where three empires meet: a narrative of recent travel in Kashmir, Western Tibet, Gilgit, and the adjoining countries.
E. F. Knight. London, New York: Longmans, Green & Co., 1893. 3rd ed. 582p. map.

Knight travelled extensively in Kashmir and what are now the Northern Areas of Pakistan in 1891, at a time when the Indian government was beginning to take a more active interest in the region. The volume contains his observations.

57 Language hunting in the Karakoram.
E. O. Lorimer. London: George Allen & Unwin, 1939. 310p.

The author was the wife of D. L. R. Lorimer (see entry no. 293), who, as a former official in the Political Department of the Government of India, had a unique opportunity in the 1930s to live in the Hunza region and to carry out further pioneering linguistic research on local languages, Burushaski in particular. This memoir describes the couple's life in the area in almost idyllic terms.

58 Forbidden journey: from Peking to Kashmir.
Ella K. Maillart. London: Heinemann, 1937. 312p. maps.

In the 1920s and 1930s, travellers continued to make their way across Central Asia to or from China, although civil war, banditry and other obstacles meant such journeys were only for the brave or foolhardy. Transport was still mostly by mule or camel, although some parts could be done by car or truck. Some of these journeys started or finished in India, and the first or last part of the trail therefore came into Kashmir via one of the passes through the high Himalayas and thence to Hunza, Gilgit and Srinagar. Two such travellers were Ella Maillart and Peter Fleming, who went from China to India in 1935. Fleming's account was published as *News from Tartary* (London: Cape, 1936), republished with another work as *Travels in Tartary* (London: Cape, 1948). Most of their writings focus on the Chinese sections of the journey, especially Turkistan, but in both cases there is a coda describing, with some relief, their arrival in Hunza and Gilgit. Other travellers who took the same route during this period included British officials. Sir Eric Teichman (*Journey to Turkistan* [London: Hodder and Stoughton, 1937]) was on a diplomatic mission to the local government of Xinjiang, while Sir Clarence (C. P.) Skrine (*Chinese Central Asia* [London: Methuen, 1926]) was a slightly earlier traveller who, as a young official, was appointed to be British consul in Kashgar. Teichman's book is particularly notable for its photographs. A more recent traveller by the same route was Stanley Stewart, whose *Frontiers of heaven* (London: John Murray, 1995) has a few pages on Hunza and Gilgit.

59 Sunset from the main.
H. G. Martin. London: Museum Press, 1951. 288p.

A wholly unselfconscious memoir by a British army officer of his sporting exploits during his long career in India. Fishing was the lure that brought him to Kashmir, while in Ladakh he hunted wild sheep and bison. A few passing comments are highly critical of Nehru and India for 'grabbing' Kashmir.

60 Abode of snow: a history of Himalayan exploration and mountaineering.
Kenneth Mason. London: Rupert Hart-Davis, 1955. 372p. bibliog.

The author was once Superintendent of the Survey of India and his book is a detailed, sometimes rather dry account both of the geology of the Himalayas and of the stages by which the region was explored and its high peaks climbed.

61 Continents in collision: the International Karakoram Project.
Keith Miller, foreword by Lord Hunt. London: George Philip, 1982. 212p. map.

This is the record of an expedition sponsored by the Royal Geographical Society of London in 1980 which brought together Pakistani, British and Chinese scientists to explore the Karakoram mountain range in the Northern Areas. The title of the book is to be taken literally, for this is an area of complex tectonic activity. The book itself, illustrated by dramatic colour photographs, is part travelogue and part report on the less specialized aspects of the scientific work of the expedition. There is a useful appendix on the history of European exploration of the area in the 19th and 20th centuries. A technical study of the same region is *Geology of Kohistan, Karakoram Himalaya, Northern Pakistan*, edited by R. A. Khan Tahirkheli, M. Qasim Jan (Peshawar, Pakistan: University of Peshawar, Centre of Excellence in Geology, c. 1979).

62 Travels in the Himalayan provinces of Hindustan and the Panjab from 1819 to 1825.
William Moorcroft, George Trebeck, introduction by G. J. Alder. Karachi, Pakistan: Oxford University Press, 1979. 2 vols. (Oxford in Asia Historical Reprints).

William Moorcroft, by training a veterinary surgeon, was one of the most remarkable of the early explorers. Keen to develop trade links with Central Asia, he made several epic journeys across the Himalayas. In 1820, he became only the second European to visit Ladakh and in fact spent several years there and in Kashmir, until in mid-1823 he left for Afghanistan *en route* to Bokhara and, ultimately, a lonely and tragic end in the desert from a fever. Although he had no high opinion of the Kashmiris, he made an intensive and valuable study of shawl-making. The present work, first published in 1841, was assembled from his papers by H. H. Wilson. Alder, who wrote the introduction to the reprint, is also the author of a comprehensive biography of Moorcroft, *Beyond Bokhara: the life of William Moorcroft, Asian explorer and pioneer veterinary surgeon, 1767-1825* (London: Century Publishing, 1985).

63 Where the Indus is young.
Dervla Murphy. London: Century Publishing, 1983. 266p. map. bibliog.

A travelogue, originally published in 1977 by a well-known practitioner of the art of travelling rough, which covers a winter spent in 1974-75 in Baltistan, part of the Northern Areas. As a woman accompanied by a young child, the author was able to see aspects of traditional Balti life that would not be open to a casual visitor. She gives lively descriptions of the scenery and of the people that she encountered.

64   Zanskar: the hidden kingdom.
Michel Peissel.   London: Collins & Harvill Press, 1979. 205p. maps.

Zanskar is a mountain range lying between Srinagar to the south and Ladakh to the north. An isolated population lives in a high valley largely cut off from the rest of the state. The people of the valley are Buddhist and share much of their culture with Ladakh and Tibet. The author, a travel writer who had made other journeys in the Himalayas, visited Zanskar in the late 1970s, only a little while after it had been opened to foreign travellers by the Indian government. The focus of the book is on the picturesque, but the reader learns a fair amount about Zanskar society. A later book, *The ants' gold* (London: Harvill Press, 1984) is an adventure story-style account of visits he made between 1980 and 1984 to Ladakh, this time to track down the legendary goldmines in the region referred to by Herodotus. He locates them, and a people called the Minaro, in the area to the east of Kargil, just north of Zanskar.

65   Between two burrs on the map: travels in northern Pakistan.
Salman Rashid.   Lahore, Pakistan: Vanguard Publications, 1995. 176p. map.

In the tradition of earlier European travellers and writers, Salman Rashid provides an amusing account of his travels from Mansehra, north of Islamabad, in a broad sweep through the mountains to Skardu, Gilgit and Chilas and eventually Chitral. Although the roads are now a little better than they were a hundred years earlier, Rashid has the same range of encounters with the local population.

66   In the throne room of the mountain gods.
Galen Rowell.   London: George Allen & Unwin, 1977. 326p.

The author was a member of the 1975 American expedition to K2. At one level this is an account of that expedition, but it is more ambitious than most such books in the way it relies on the diaries of the individual participants to paint the picture of the successes and failures of the expedition (including the failure to reach the summit). Rowell also writes engagingly on the past history of attempts on the mountain.

67   That untravelled world: an autobiography.
Eric Shipton.   London: Hodder & Stoughton, 1969. 286p. maps.

The autobiography of a renowned mountaineer who made some of the interwar attempts to climb Mount Everest. He made a major expedition to the Karakoram in 1937, to which a separate chapter of this book is devoted. He also described the expedition in *Blank on the map* (London: Hodder & Stoughton, 1938).

68   Words for my brother: travels between the Hindu Kush and the Himalayas.
John Staley.   Karachi, Pakistan: Oxford University Press, 1982. 287p. maps. bibliog.

The author is a professional geographer who visited the Northern Areas on a number of occasions to conduct research on glaciers but who at the same time became fascinated by the lives of the people who lived in these remote areas. This book tries, through the author's own experiences and his research, to convey the spirit of their lives, as well as to sketch in the development of their relations with the wider world.

69 The golden oriole: childhood, family and friends in India.
Raleigh Trevelyan.   London: Secker & Warburg, 1987. 536p. map.
bibliog.

A member of the famous Trevelyan family, many of whom had distinguished careers as
British officials in India, the author was born in India and returned on a number of
occasions after independence to write this sensitive memoir in which direct observation
mingles with reminiscence and family history. There are extensive sections devoted to the
valley, in particular to Gulmarg, where the family had spent summers in the 1920s, and
to Gilgit.

70 Travels in Kashmir, Ladak, Iskardo, the countries adjoining the mountain-course of the Indus, and the Himalaya, north of the Panjab.
G. T. Vigne.   London: Henry Colburn, 1842. 2 vols. map.

Vigne travelled extensively in Kashmir and the Western Himalaya during the second half
of the 1830s. Although Moorcroft (see entry no. 62) had preceded him, he was the first
European to visit Skardu and to explore the Baltistan region in any depth. He appears the
archetypal English amateur, with his concern for hunting and for the local topography,
although John Keay (see entry no. 55) suggests he may also have worked as a British
agent.

71 Early Jesuit travellers in Central Asia, 1603-1721.
C. Wessels.   The Hague: Martinus Nijhoff, 1924. 344p. map. bibliog.

In the 17th century a number of Jesuit priests made their way, usually perilously, to Tibet,
in order to seek converts to their faith. Although the main emphasis of their journals and
writings was on Tibet itself, several of them passed through Kashmir and recorded their
impressions, notably Ippolito Desideri, who left early accounts of both Srinagar and Leh,
where he was the first recorded European visitor. Wessels' book summarizes Desideri's
journey, while his journal has also been published – *An account of Tibet: the travels of
Ippolito Desideri of Pistoia, SJ., 1712-1727*, edited by Filippo de Filippi, with an
introduction by C. Wessels (London: George Routledge, 1932 [The Broadway
Travellers]). The earliest European visitors to Kashmir, Fathers Jerome Xavier and
Benoist de Goës, who visited the region in 1597, were also Jesuits. The account of their
travels by Pierre du Jarric (*Akbar and the Jesuits: an account of the Jesuit missionaries
to the court of Akbar*, translated by C. H. Payne [London: Routledge, 1926]) is not
particularly detailed or illuminating. A secondary work is Edward Maclagan, *The Jesuits
and the great Mogul* (London: Burns, Oates & Washbourne, 1932).

Tourism

72   India handbook.
Robert Bradnock, Roma Bradnock.   Bath, England: Footprint
Handbooks, 1996. 6th ed. 1,470p. maps. bibliog.
Originally published as *South Asian handbook* in 1991, this is an annually updated
guidebook. It includes the standard information on places to see, hotels, transport, etc.,
but compared to many other guidebooks it is particularly strong on the historical and
geographical context. The maps are also of a very high quality. Forty-two pages are
devoted to Jammu and Kashmir, and the authors are careful to indicate those areas that
are safe to visit.

**73   A handbook for travellers in India, Pakistan, Nepal, Bangladesh
and Sri Lanka (Ceylon).**
L. F. Rushbrook Williams.   London: John Murray, 1975. 22nd ed.
(reprinted with amendments, 1982). 762p. maps. bibliog.
Often known as Murray's Guide, this is by far the oldest extant tourist guide for South
Asia, dating back to the 19th century, and is in some ways a historical curiosity. There is
a separate section on Kashmir that only barely accepts the reality of the present division
of the state, and lists the pre-1947 routes into the valley.

74   Kashmir, Ladakh and Zanskar.
Margret Schettler, Rolf Schettler.   South Yarra, Victoria: Lonely
Planet Publications, 1989. 176p. maps.
The standard guide for budget travellers, written in the usual Lonely Planet style with
down-to-earth advice based on the direct experience of the authors. The book does not
cover Azad Kashmir or Pakistan's Northern Areas. The political crisis in Kashmir means
that there has been no edition since 1989. However, the Lonely Planet company continues
to publish other guides that cover the Kashmir area in part: *Karakoram highway* (John
King, Bradley Mayhew, 1998. 3rd ed.); *Indian Himalaya* (Bradley Mayhew et al., 1999.
2nd ed.); *Trekking in the Indian Himalaya* (Garry Weare, 1996. 3rd ed.). The country

guides for India (Christine Niven et al., 1999. 8th ed.) and Pakistan (John King et al., 1998. 5th ed.) are also useful.

75 The trekker's guide to the Himalaya and Karakoram.
Hugh Swift.   San Francisco: Sierra Club Books, 1982. 342p. maps. bibliog.

Covers the whole of the Himalayan region and contains four chapters describing in detail treks that can be made in Gilgit, Baltistan, Kashmir and Ladakh respectively. The approach is sensible, and there are useful chapters giving a wide range of practical information. There are also glossaries of several of the local languages and a chapter on flora and fauna.

History

General

76 Kashmir: beyond the vale.
M. J. Akbar.   Delhi: Viking, 1991. 232p. map. bibliog.
M. J. Akbar is a senior Indian journalist who has written extensively on the challenges facing India. He believes strongly that Kashmiri culture is characterized by harmony and mutual respect, and the first part of this book ranges widely across political and cultural history to illustrate the point. In the second part he discusses in greater detail the history of events from 1947 to the point when he was writing at the beginning of the insurgency. He attempts, from what might be called a liberal Indian position, to understand the motives of all the major participants.

77 Culture and political history of Kashmir.
P. N. K. Bamzai.   Delhi: MD Publications, 1994. 3 vols. 882p. (continuous pagination). bibliog.
A scholarly overview in narrative style by one of the longest established figures in the field of the whole of Kashmir's political and cultural history. The tone as a whole is measured and judicious, although towards the end the author clearly writes from an Indian perspective and makes no secret of his admiration for the tough approach on law and order adopted by Jagmohan, twice governor of the state (see entry no. 256). Volume one covers the period up to the 14th century, volume two up to the beginning of the 19th century, and volume three right up to the present. Bamzai is the author of many other general works on Kashmiri history, for example *Socio-economic history of Kashmir (1846-1925)* (Delhi: Metropolitan, 1987).

78 Ladakhi history and Indian nationhood.
John Bray.   *South Asia Research*, vol. 11, no. 2 (1991), p. 115-33. bibliog.
A succinct and reliable account of Ladakh's history and current politics in the light of recent tensions, especially those produced by the Kashmir insurgency. Ladakhi Buddhists

in particular are concerned about their position in any future autonomous or independent Kashmir state. Bray ends his article with a brief note on possible political futures for Ladakh.

79 The Cambridge history of India.
London: Cambridge University Press, 1922-37. 5 vols. maps. bibliog.

The *Cambridge history of India* was planned to include six volumes, although the second volume on the later classical period was never written. The contributors and editors were a mixture of professional academics and scholar-administrators. While still valuable as a reference work in some areas, it has for the most part been overtaken by modern scholarship. Volume 1 (published in 1922 and edited by E. J. Rapson) deals with ancient India, volume 3 (1928, edited by Wolseley Haig) with the Turks and Afghans, volume 4 (1937, edited by Richard Burn) with the Mughal period, volume 5 (1929, edited by H. H. Dodwell) with British India, 1497-1858, and vol. 6 (1932, edited by H. H. Dodwell) with the Indian empire, 1858-1918. In India, the *History and culture of the Indian people*, edited by R. C. Majumdar and produced under the auspices of the Bharatiya Vidya Bhavan, an organization devoted to promoting Indian culture (Bombay, 1951-69), offers a similar breadth of view. A *New Cambridge history of India* has begun to appear, but this comprises a series of monographs on interconnected topics rather than the synoptic volumes of the earlier work. Many of these touch, or will touch, on Kashmir – for example, the volume on *The Sikhs of the Punjab* by J. S. Grewal (Cambridge: Cambridge University Press, 1990), and the forthcoming volumes on Indian sufism by Bruce Lawrence and the princely states by Barbara Ramusack.

80 Historical tales of Kashmir.
Somnath Dhar.   Delhi: Sagar Publications, 1983. 132p.

A collection of vignettes of figures in Kashmir's history, retold in a popular and didactic style. Some of the stories border on folktales (Dhar has written other similar folklore collections).

81 The story of Kashmir: yesterday and today.
Edited by Verinder Grover.   Delhi: Deep & Deep Publications, 1995. 3 vols. bibliog.

These volumes consist in the main of reprinted articles and extracts from books relating to Kashmir's political history. The first volume covers the period up to independence, and includes cultural as well as political issues, while the second takes the account up to 1994. Both include chronologies. The final volume includes a number of key documents and an extensive, but unannotated, bibliography. A similar work by Grover and Ranjana Arora, *Indian government and politics at crossroads: political instability, money, power and corruption, Punjab and Kashmir problems, secularism, religion and politics, development towards 2000 AD* (Delhi: Deep & Deep Publications, 1995. 1,106p. bibliog. [Development of Politics and Government in India, no. 10]) includes several of the same pieces on Kashmir. Both are valuable collections, although their scholarly usefulness is severely restricted by the failure to indicate the original location of the articles.

82   The Muslims of British India.
Peter Hardy.   London: Cambridge University Press, 1972. 306p.
maps. bibliog. (Cambridge South Asian Studies, no. 13).

This masterly work surveys the historical experience of the Muslims of South Asia from
the decline of Mughal power to what the author describes as the dual partition, the
division of India into two sovereign states and of the Muslim population between them.
He outlines the main intellectual trends both among those exposed to the colonial
educational institutions and among those who remained within the traditional framework
of the religious seminary, and discusses the ways in which Muslims entered politics, for
what purposes, and with what success. Although Kashmiri Muslims are excluded from
the story of British India, their experience relates in many respects to that of their co-
religionists outside the state.

83   Reclaiming the past: the search for political and cultural unity in contemporary Jammu and Kashmir.
Vernon Hewitt.   London: Portland Books, 1995. 212p. maps. bibliog.

A brief history of the state since pre-colonial times, written with an eye to the political
crisis of the 1990s. The author is sympathetic to the Indian view of the situation, and
argues that despite India's past mistakes, an 'internal' solution based on the existing line
of control remains the best hope for lasting peace. He emphasizes the cultural diversity of
the people of the region and argues that this diversity would be in danger if Kashmir were
to achieve independence or join Pakistan.

84   Kashmir sold and resold.
S. M. Jaffar.   Lahore, Pakistan: Book Traders, 1992. 324p. bibliog.

This book offers an extended account of the Kashmir dispute in historical perspective
from the Pakistani point of view.

85   Free Kashmir.
Amanullah Khan.   Karachi, Pakistan: Central Printing Press, 1970.
222p. bibliog. map.

Amanullah Khan was one of the founders of the Jammu and Kashmir Liberation Front
(JKLF) in 1965 and emerged as the leader of one of its two main factions. In this book,
he reviews Kashmir's history and the events of 1947 before calling for an independent
Kashmir, a development which he considers would lead to better relations within the
whole South Asia region.

86   Kashmir past and present: unravelling the mystique.
Mohan Lal Koul.   Delhi: Sehyog Prakashan, 1994. 242p.

A vehement attack on the record of Muslim rulers and leaders in Kashmir from the 13th
century to the 1990s. While praising the tolerance of individual figures, such as the 15th-
century ruler Sultan Zain-ul-Abidin, and Bakshi Ghulam Mohammad, the chief minister
who replaced Sheikh Abdullah in 1953, the general record is seen as extraordinarily
bleak.

87 Kashmir: a disputed legacy 1846-1990.

Alastair Lamb.   Hertingfordbury, England: Roxford Books, 1991.
368p. maps. bibliog.

Although some aspects of his analysis are hotly disputed, Lamb is one of the leading scholars of Kashmir, especially within the geostrategic context of Central Asia. His aim in the present work, which sums up nearly a lifetime's work on the region and revises some of his earlier formulations, is to trace the history of Jammu and Kashmir first as a princely state and then after 1947, and to discuss its changing geostrategic significance. While this was of central importance in understanding the 19th-century history of the region, he regards it as no longer significant. He also emphasizes the importance of looking at the state as made up of different communities. Earlier relevant books by Lamb are *Crisis in Kashmir* (London: Routledge & Kegan Paul, 1966) and *The Sino-Indian Border in Ladakh* (Canberra: Australian National University Press, 1973).

88 The Indian Muslims.

M. Mujeeb.   London: George Allen & Unwin, 1967. 590p. bibliog.

This is perhaps the most authoritative account of the history of South Asia's Muslims from the 'nationalist Muslim' point of view. Mujeeb is concerned to depict the various ways in which, over time, Muslims have defined themselves and their distinctive position in Indian society. This takes him into the social, political, and artistic, as well as the religious fields. There are only occasional references to Kashmiri Muslims, but they fit well into his general frame of analysis.

89 Kashmir: from crisis to crisis.

Nasir A. Naqash, G. M. Shah.   Delhi: APH Publishing Corporation, 1997. 171p. bibliog.

A general study by two Kashmiri academics based at the University of Srinagar and broadly sympathetic to the plight of the local population. This work combines a brief historical account of the period from 1846 to the present, with some wider general analysis of the genesis of the 1990s crisis. The authors present an account that is critical of some actions of the Indian government but which identifies other factors as well. Another study from an academic at the University of Srinagar, this time more specifically focused on political history from 1931 to the present day, is *Kashmir politics: problems and prospects* by Gul Mohd. Wani (Delhi: Ashish Publishing House, 1993).

90 Cultural heritage of the Dogras.

Jyoteeshwar Pathik.   Delhi: Light and Life Publishers, 1980. 177p.
bibliog.

In this book, the author presents an overview of Jammu's history and culture, offering a sympathetic treatment of the Dogra dynasty that ruled in the 19th and 20th centuries. Based on an eclectic range of sources, Pathik covers the political history of the region from early times and gives brief accounts of the arts, festivals and local customs.

91 The Muslim community of the Indo-Pakistan subcontinent (610-1947): a brief historical analysis.
Ishtiaq Husain Qureshi. Karachi, Pakistan: Ma'aref, 1977. 2nd ed. 385p. bibliog.

First published in 1962, this work has become a standard Pakistani account of the country's history, seen as part of the history of the Muslims of the subcontinent as a whole. Qureshi begins with the first Arab traders and moves on through the Muslim dynasties and the decline of Muslim political power to the rise of the Muslim League, the Khilafat movement (described by him as an 'adventure in altruism') and the Pakistan movement itself. Kashmir is covered, although not to any extent in the 20th century.

92 Special status in Indian federalism: Jammu and Kashmir.
Hari Ram. Delhi: Seema Publications, 1983. 230p. bibliog.

This is a political rather than a constitutional study. It discusses the way the special status of Jammu and Kashmir within the Indian Union has operated in practice, and draws attention to its implications for relations between Kashmir on the one hand and Jammu and Ladakh on the other.

93 Wars and no peace over Kashmir.
Maroof Raza. Delhi: Lancer Publishers; London: Spantech & Lancer, 1996. 179p. maps. bibliog.

A former officer in the Indian army who has become a strategic analyst, Maroof Raza's useful work consists of a series of essays on the Kashmir issue from before independence until the present day. While in general accepting the legitimacy of India's position, he writes sympathetically of the strains and difficulties that have led to the rise of militancy, as well as of the difficulties that hamper any proposed solution.

94 Islam in the Indian subcontinent.
Annemarie Schimmel. Leiden, the Netherlands: E. J. Brill, 1980. 303p. bibliog. (Handbuch der Orientalistik, 2 Abteilung, 4 Band, 3 Abschnitt).

A good general account of Islam in the Indian subcontinent, by one of the leading Western authorities on the subject. There is a succinct section on medieval Kashmir, as well as other references. Another excellent source for Islam in South Asia is by Aziz Ahmad, *Studies in Islamic culture in the Indian environment* (Oxford: Clarendon Press, 1964). Aziz Ahmad sees the development of an Islamic culture in India both as a regional formulation of a general Islamic culture and as a process of interaction with the Hinduism that is indigenous to the region. These themes are directly relevant to the Kashmiri case.

95 Kashmir in conflict: India, Pakistan and the unfinished war.
Victoria Schofield. London: I. B. Tauris, 2000. 286p. maps. bibliog.

A general introduction to the Kashmir issue from before independence to the 1990s by a sympathetic and well-informed journalist. She covers the controversy over the events of 1947 with considerable skill. The book intertwines accounts of the dispute between India and Pakistan with an analysis of the internal politics of Indian-held Kashmir. Although it is not clear from the title page, the book is in fact a heavily revised version of the author's earlier *Kashmir in the crossfire* (London: I. B. Tauris, 1996). The new version has less on the earlier history and more on the contemporary situation.

96 Converted Kashmir.
Narender Sehgal. Delhi: Utpal Publications, 1994. 474p. bibliog.

Complete with a foreword by the head of the Hindu nationalist organization, the Rashtriya Swayamsevak Sangh (RSS), this is an overtly 'Hindu' view of Kashmir history and of the present crisis. The first section extols Kashmiri civilization in the ancient period; the second claims that Muslim rulers used force to convert the population to Islam, while the Pandits were cruelly oppressed; the third claims that Sheikh Abdullah was a British agent, and that subsequent leaders of Kashmir such as Farooq Abdullah were anti-Hindu and maintained covert links with pro-Pakistan groups; while the final section sees the post-1989 crisis as a proxy war waged by Pakistan.

97 Pakistan occupied Kashmir: under the jackboot.
Edited by Jasjit Singh. Delhi: Siddhi Books, 1995. 219p. map.

As the title indicates, this is hardly a dispassionate analysis of the political situation in the part of Jammu and Kashmir presently controlled by Pakistan, but the contributors are all well-informed Indian journalists and analysts. One chapter deals with the historical position of Gilgit and Baltistan (and includes the text of the lease of Gilgit in 1935 and the Sino-Pakistan frontier agreement of 1963), and one with their more recent political and constitutional history, while two deal in a similar manner with Azad Kashmir itself. A final chapter relates more general trends in Pakistan to those in Azad Kashmir and the Northern Areas.

98 A history of India: volume two.
Percival Spear. Harmondsworth, England: Penguin Books, 1965. 284p. maps. bibliog.

A standard history of the Indian subcontinent for the general reader, written by a British historian of humanist and liberal persuasions. The first volume of the history, by Romila Thapar (Harmondsworth, England: Penguin Books, 1966), covers the classical period and the early Muslim dynasties. Jammu, Kashmir and the other northern areas are only occasionally the centre of attention, but the overall framework offered is valuable.

99 Kashir.
G. M. D. Sufi. Delhi: Light and Life Publishers, 1974. 2 vols. 832p. (continuous pagination; appendix and index separately paginated.)

The author offers a lengthy account of Kashmir's history and culture from their origins up to 1925. Each dynasty is given its own chapter or section. There is little secondary analysis in this work, but it is important for its coverage of the original sources in Persian and other languages, although the extracts are not translated. Besides the political history chapters, there are sections on poetry and literature, on handicrafts, and on miscellaneous topics such as roads, weights and measures and numismatics.

100   Jammu and Kashmir at the political crossroads.
P. S. Verma.   Delhi: Vikas Publishing House, 1994. 296p.
This book attempts an overview of politics in Kashmir since 1947. There are extensive reviews of electoral politics up to 1989 and of the legislative elite in the state. The final chapter is devoted to an analysis of the 1989 uprising and the militant groups. Verma sees the prime responsibility resting with Pakistani machinations, but recognizes that internal problems also played a part in provoking the troubles.

101   India, Pakistan, and the Kashmir dispute: on regional conflict and its resolution.
Robert Wirsing.   London: Macmillan, 1994. 337p. maps. bibliog.
A very competent review of the complexities of the problem and possible solutions. Wirsing provides a succinct summary of the origins of the dispute and of the strategic context, followed by a discussion of the 1989 uprising and the Indian government's response, before moving on to examine possible models for a solution. A similar but shorter piece by Wirsing is *War or peace on the line of control? The India-Pakistan dispute over Kashmir turns fifty* (Durham, England: International Boundaries Research Unit, 1998 [Boundary and Territorial Briefing, vol. 2, no. 5]).

Pre-colonial (up to 1846)

102   The Akbarnāma.
Abu-l-Fazl, translated by H. Beveridge.   Calcutta, India: Asiatic Society of Bengal, 1899-1939. 3 vols. (Bibliotheca Indica).
This massive Persian work, which in translation runs to well over 2,000 pages, is the official biography of the emperor Akbar by Abul Fazl, his principal administrator. While the literary form is that of a court biography, including, for example, minute astrological details, it remains one of the most important sources available for Mughal history. The edition, although old, is scholarly. The third volume includes a detailed account of Akbar's conquest of Kashmir in 1586 and his visits in 1589 and subsequently. The final part of the *Akbarnama*, the *'Ain-i-Ākbari*, gives a detailed account of the government and economic conditions of the Mughal empire under Akbar. It is always treated as a separate work. The standard translation is still that of H. Blochmann and H. S. Jarrett (Calcutta, India: Asiatic Society of Bengal, 1873-94. 3 vols.).

103   Central Asia and Western Himalaya: a forgotten link.
Edited by Ghulam Mohd. Buth.   Jodhpur, India: Scientific Publishers, 1986. 79p. maps. bibliog.
A collection of scholarly papers on the neolithic period, despite the title mainly with reference to the Kashmir region. There is a special emphasis on the initial development of agriculture.

104 Jammu kingdom.
Sukhdev Singh Charak.   Delhi: Light and Life Publishers, 1980.
421p. maps. bibliog. (History and Culture of Himalayan States, vol.
V, part II).
This a careful historical treatment of the rise of Jammu state from one of many small hill
states in the region to the dominant force within the declining Sikh state of Ranjit Singh
and, eventually, in 1846 to control of Kashmir and surrounding areas. Charak gives due
weight to economic and geographical factors, and includes an account of Zorawar Singh's
adventures in Ladakh and Tibet. Appendices give the texts of important documents.

105 Ladakh and Western Himalayan politics, 1819-1848: the Dogra conquest of Ladakh, Baltistan and West Tibet and reactions of other powers.
C. L. Datta.   Delhi: Munshiram Manoharlal Publishers, 1973. 239p.
map. bibliog.
The Dogra conquest of Ladakh, under the Dogra ruler Gulab Singh and his principal
military leader General Zorawar Singh, was a key aspect of the subsequent creation of the
state of Jammu and Kashmir. The present work is a careful analysis of the geopolitics of
the region in the 18th and 19th centuries, as local interests, for example of the rising
Gurkha state in Nepal, intersected with the ambitions of the British and Russian states.
Zorawar Singh's remarkable military successes were brought to a halt with his defeat and
death when he overreached himself with an invasion of Western Tibet. Datta has also
written his biography (*General Zorawar Singh: his life and achievements in Ladakh,
Baltistan and Tibet* (Delhi: Deep & Deep Publications, 1984).

106 A history of Ladakh.
August Hermann Francke. Introduction and notes by S. S. Gergan, F.
M. Hassnain.   Delhi: Sterling Publishers, 1977. 182p. maps.
Francke was a member of the Moravian mission to Ladakh founded in the late 19th
century. He made a major contribution to the study of the Tibetan language, as well as
writing the first systematic history of Ladakh. His book was originally published in 1907
under the title *A history of western Tibet: one of the unknown empires*.

107 The great Moghuls.
Bamber Gascoigne.   London: Jonathan Cape, 1971. 264p. map.
bibliog.
This is an extensively illustrated popular account of the Mughal emperors. Separate
chapters are devoted to Babur, Humayun, Akbar, Jahangir, Shah Jahan and Aurangzeb.
Kashmir features as their favourite escape from the heat, dust and conflict of the plains.

108 Rashīd al-Dīn's *History of India*: collected essays with facsimiles and indices.
Karl Jahn.   The Hague: Mouton, 1965. 119p. (Central Asiatic
Studies, no. 10).
Rashid al-Din was vizier to a Mongol prince at the end of the 13th century, and under his
instructions wrote what was in effect a universal history, one section of which deals with

India. Although much of the material derives from Al-Biruni (an early Arab traveller who wrote a remarkable book on Indian history and culture), the passages on Kashmir derive from the work of another writer, Kamalashri, known only from this secondary source. One of the essays in the present volume is entitled 'A note on Kashmir and the Mongols'. Jahn has also translated the text of the *History of India* into German (*Die Indiengeschichte des Rašīd ad-Dīn: Einleitung, Vollständige Übersetzung, Kommentar und 80 Texttafeln* [Rashid ad-Din's History of India: introduction, complete translation, commentary and 80 facsimile reproductions] [Vienna: Verlag der Österreichischen Akademie der Wissenschaften, 1980]).

109 Antiquities of northern Pakistan: reports and studies.
Edited by Karl Jettmar. Mainz am Rhein, Germany: Verlag Philipp von Zabern, 1989-94. 3 vols. bibliog.

The petroglyphs or rock carvings along the Indus valley in its upper reaches along the ancient trade routes have only become fully known in recent years. Dating back to at least the third millennium BCE, they are a major source for the prehistoric and Buddhist periods. These volumes of essays by European and Pakistani scholars have been brought together by the leading specialist on the subject. The second part of the first volume, printed separately, is devoted to photographic illustrations of the carvings. A related volume of photographs and text, produced originally for an exhibition and intended for a general readership, is *Between Gandhara and the silk road: rock-carvings along the Karakoram highway. Discoveries by German-Pakistani expeditions, 1979-1984*, edited by Karl Jettmar, Volker Thewalt (Mainz am Rhein, Germany: Verlag Philipp von Zabern, 1987).

110 Bolor: a contribution to the political and ethnic geography of North Pakistan.
Karl Jettmar. *Zentralasiatische Studien*, 11 (1977), p. 411-448.

Using a wide range of sources, especially in Chinese, the author seeks to unravel the history of the Gilgit region in the first and early second millennia CE. He identifies Bolor, often mentioned in the Chinese sources, with the Gilgit and Baltistan areas, and proposes locations for other names to be found in the Chinese sources. He also speculates about the ethnic identity of their populations.

111 Ex moneta: essays on numismatics, history and archaeology in honour of Dr. David W. Macdowell.
Edited by Amal Kumar Jha, Sanjay Garg. Delhi: Harman Publishing House, 1998. 2 vols.

Two articles in this large collection relate to Kashmir. Nicholas Rhodes writes on 'Some problematic coins of the Kashmir Sultan', which focuses on the 16th century, and Karl Jettmar in 'No coins from Gilgit' uses the paucity of coin finds from the Gilgit area to explore the likely structure of government and society in the pre-colonial era. The pre-Mughal medieval period is also covered in an article by John Deyell in a collection edited by John Richards, *The imperial monetary system of Mughal India* (Delhi: Oxford University Press, 1987).

112 The history and culture of Kashmir.
M. L. Kapur.   Delhi: Anmol Publications, 1992. 356p. bibliog.

This covers the history of Kashmir from the first reliable historical records in the 8th century CE to its absorption into the Mughal empire in 1586. The author relies on the standard published sources such as the chronicles to produce a well-integrated and readable, although still fairly dry, account. An earlier version was published as *Studies in history and culture of Kashmir* (Jammu, India: Kashmir History Publications, 1980. 2nd ed.).

113 De Geschriften van Francisco Pelsaert over Mughal Indië, 1627. Kroniek en Remonstrantie. (Francisco Pelsaert's writings on Mughal India, 1627. Chronicle and report.)
Edited by D. H. A. Kolff, H. W. van Santen.   The Hague: Martinus Nijhoff, 1979. 361p. map. bibliog. (Werken uitgegeven door de Linschoten-Vereeniging, 81).

Francisco Pelsaert was an officer of the Dutch East India Company who worked in India from 1620 to 1627. Based at Agra, he saw a great deal of the Mughal emperor Jahangir. The *Remonstrantie* is a report on the commercial conditions of the time, and includes a section on Kashmir, while the chronicle is a history of the Mughals from Humayun to Jahangir. This scholarly edition includes an extended introduction. The *Remonstrantie* is available in an English translation by W. H. Moreland and P. Geyl, *Jahangir's India: the* Remonstrantie *of Francisco Pelsaert* (Cambridge, England: Heffer, 1925).

114 The Subah of Kashmir under the later Mughals (1708-1748).
Zahiruddin Malik.   In: *Medieval India: a miscellany, volume 2.* Edited by K. A. Nizami.   Bombay, India: Asia Publishing House, 1972, p. 249-62.

Malik's detailed political history of Kashmir in this period depicts the 18th century as a time of anarchy. Oppressive rule often provoked revolts and sectarian strife, while the region also felt the impact of problems elsewhere, for example Nadir Shah's invasion of India.

115 Mughals in India: a bibliographical survey. vol. 1. Manuscripts.
D. N. Marshall.   London: Asia Publishing House, 1967. 634p.

The compiler has attempted to include all manuscripts, whatever the language, which are relevant to the study of political, economic and social conditions during the Mughal period. Items therefore range from the well known, for example the ʿAin-i-Akbari (see entry no. 102), to minor works that may nevertheless be highly relevant to one particular area or topic. Each of the 2,105 entries is annotated. The entries are arranged by author's name and there are title and subject indices. Over fifty items relate to Kashmir. The work was reprinted in 1985 as *Mughals in India: a bibliographical survey of manuscripts* (London: Mansell).

116 Kashmir under the Mughals, 1586-1752.
Abdul Majid Mattoo. Srinagar, India: Golden Horde Enterprises,
1988. 272p. bibliog.
Divided into sections on politics, society and economy, this book aims at a general
coverage of the period, based on the original Persian sources. The author offers a positive
assessment of the period.

**117 Early medieval history of Kashmir (with special reference to the
Loharas) A.D. 1003-1171.**
Krishna Mohan. Delhi: Meharchand Lachhmandas Publications,
1981. 386p. map. bibliog.
Originally written in the 1950s as a PhD thesis, this is a detailed study of Kashmir during
the Lohara dynasty, which ruled in the 11th and 12th centuries. Chapters are devoted to
Kashmir's relations with neighbouring states, administrative structure, social relations,
particularly the question of whether society was 'feudal', and to religious beliefs and
practices. The major source for the study is the *Rajatarangini* (see entry no. 124), and the
author devotes some space to discussing its reliability, which she rates highly.

118 Bahāristān-i-shāhī: a chronicle of mediaeval Kashmir.
Edited by K. N. Pandit. Calcutta, India: Firma KLM, 1991. 296p.
bibliog.
This is one of a number of Persian histories of Kashmir produced during the medieval
period, in this case by an unknown author in the early 17th century. While most of the text
concerns political history, it is possible to learn much about social structure and other
topics, especially from the early 14th century on. The translator has added a useful
introduction.

119 The kingdom of Ladakh c.950-1842 A.D.
Luciano Petech. Rome: Instituto italiano per il Medio ed Estrema
Oriente, 1977. 191p. bibliog. (Rome Oriental Series, no. 51).
This is a comprehensive political and dynastic history of Ladakh from the earliest known
records to the kingdom's final collapse at the hands of the Dogras in 1842. The author
uses the full range of Tibetan and other sources. These are more complete for the period
after the 15th century, and the work's coverage reflects this.

**120 The wonder that was India, vol. II. A survey of the history and
culture of the Indian sub-continent from the coming of the
Muslims to the British conquest.**
S. A. A. Rizvi. London: Sidgwick & Jackson, 1987. 416p. maps.
bibliog.
Rizvi is a well-known writer on many aspects of medieval Indian Muslim history, and this
work draws extensively on his detailed knowledge of Islamic movements, especially the
sufi orders, for example the *Kubrawiyya*, who played a significant role in medieval
Kashmir. The *Kubrawiyya* are also the subject of an extended article by M. Molé, 'Les
Kubrawiya entre sunnisme et shiisme aux huitième et neuvième siècles de l'Hégire'
(Between Sunnism and Shiism, the Kubrawiyya in the 8th and 9th centuries AH) in the

Revue des Études Islamiques, vol. 29 (1961). Rizvi's book is a sequel to the same publisher's *The wonder that was India* by A. L. Basham (1967. 3rd ed.), which has some references to Kashmir in the classical period.

121 Political history of Kashmir (B. C. 300-A. D. 1200).
K. S. Saxena. Lucknow, India: Upper India Publishing House, 1974. 364p. maps. bibliog.

Despite the title, most of this study, which was originally a PhD thesis, is devoted to the period from the rise of the Karkota dynasty in the 8th century. Before that time, the available material is very scanty, although Saxena does his best to extract a coherent story. Thereafter he depends heavily on the *Rajatarangini* (see entry no. 124) for his account of the Karkota and subsequent dynasties.

122 Kashmir: history and archaeology through the ages.
S. L. Shali. Delhi: Indus Publishing Company, 1993. 311p. map. bibliog.

Based on a wide variety of academic sources, this is an overview of the archaeology and history of the Kashmir region from the palaeolithic period to the 19th century. For the later periods, the coverage is mainly in terms of architectural monuments, although there are brief summaries of political events. The book contains sixty-five black-and-white photographs of archaeological sites, sculptures and buildings.

123 Kashmir under the Sikhs.
Dewan Chand Sharma. Delhi: Seema Publications, 1983. 333p. map. bibliog.

Originally a thesis, this comprehensive work concentrates on economic and social conditions during the Sikh period of rule in Kashmir, which lasted from 1819 to 1846. The author relies heavily on unpublished material collected by William Moorcroft (see entry no. 62) and also uses Persian material. A work that covers the same ground is *A history of Sikh rule in Kashmir 1819-1846*, by R. K. Parmu (Srinagar, India: Government of Jammu and Kashmir, Department of Education, 1977).

124 Kalhaṇa's Rājataraṅgiṇī, a chronicle of the Kings of Kaśmīr.
Edited and translated by M. A. Stein. London: Archibald Constable, 1900. 2 vols.

The *Rajatarangini*, written in the middle of the 12th century CE, is a unique example in South Asia of a historical chronicle, and is the most important source for the early history of the Kashmir region. Kalhana was from a family which had earlier held senior court positions, and his description of the most recent dynasties is probably based on personal knowledge, while the earlier sections bring together traditional accounts. The standard English translation and commentary is by Sir Aurel Stein, who had earlier published the Sanskrit text. The two-volume work includes an extensive and scholarly introduction and an equally important memoir of the ancient geography of Kashmir, as well as the translated text. Another frequently cited translation is by Nehru's brother-in-law, Ranjit Sitaram Pandit (Allahabad, India: Indian Press, 1935). This lacks the full scholarly apparatus of the Stein edition but the translation is more readable. Both translations have been reprinted, Stein's by Motilal Banarsidass (Delhi, 1988) and Pandit's by the Sahitya Akademi (Delhi, 1968). There is an important article on the *Rajatarangini* by A. L.

Basham in *Historians of India, Pakistan and Ceylon* (Edited by C. H. Philips. London: Oxford University Press, 1961. [Historical Writing on the Peoples of Asia, no. 1]). Other articles in the same volume also comment on it.

125 **Eine Lebensbeschreibung des Scheichs ʿAlī-i Hamadānī (gestorben 1385): Die *Xulāṣat ul-Manāqib* des Maulānā Nūr ud-Dīn Caʿfar-i Badaxšī.** (A description of the life of Sheikh Ali-i Hamadani (died 1385): the *Xulasat ul-Manaqib* of Maulana Nur ud-Din Jafar-i Badakshi.)
J. K. Teufel. Leiden, the Netherlands: E. J. Brill, 1962. 157p. bibliog.

Sheikh Hamadani was the founder of a sufi order and played a major role in the early Islamization of Kashmir during visits in 1379-82 and 1384. The present edition includes a translation of the text, but the main references to the early Islamic history of Kashmir are to be found in the introductory material. There is an article on Hamadani in *The encyclopaedia of Islam* (see entry no. 308).

126 **Muslim rule in Kashmir (1554 AD to 1586 AD).**
Nizam-ud-Din Wani.   Delhi: Anmol Publications, 1993. 308p. bibliog.

Originally a thesis, this is a detailed, scholarly study of the Chak dynasty, which ruled Kashmir from 1554 CE until the region's conquest by the Mughal emperor Akbar in 1586. Persian and Kashmiri manuscript sources have been extensively used. The author portrays the Chak rulers, with the exception of the last, as humane and liberal-minded. The work covers the complex political history of the period as the Mughal empire expanded, and also more general questions of administration, economic conditions and cultural life.

Colonial

127 **A collection of treaties, engagements and sanads relating to India and neighbouring countries. Vol. 11, The treaties, &c. relating to the North-West Frontier Province, Baluchistan, Jammu and Kashmir, Eastern Turkistan and Afghanistan.**
C. U. Aitchison.   Calcutta, India: Superintendent Government Printing, 1909. 393p. maps.

Aitchison's collection is the standard source for the treaties that regulated the British Crown's relations with the Indian princes. Volume 11 contains the text of the treaty of Amritsar and a number of subsequent agreements, together with documents relating to Gilgit and Hunza. The texts are preceded by a summary of their contents and the constitutional position as it was understood by the British.

128 British India's northern frontier 1865-95: a study in imperial policy.
G. J. Alder.   London: Longmans, 1963. 392p. maps. bibliog.
(Imperial Studies Series, no. 25).

This is a careful and detailed study of the northern rather than the north-west frontier of India, stretching from the Pamirs to the eastern end of the Karakoram range. The author examines the attempts to control the region during the 19th century by both the Russians and the British. Eventually, after many alarms and excursions involving soldiers, diplomats and explorers, an agreement was signed in 1895 that settled the spheres of influence of the two sides. Alder also discusses the involvement of China in the area. There is a detailed account of the early history of the Gilgit Agency.

129 Lives of the Indian princes.
Charles Allen, Sharada Dwivedi.   London: Century Publishing, 1984. 352p. map.

A coffee-table book which uses extensive interview material, including significant contributions from Karan Singh, the son of Maharaja Hari Singh, the last ruler of Kashmir. There is a discreet reference to the notorious Mr A case from the 1920s, in which Maharaja Hari Singh was the victim of a blackmail plot during a visit to London.

130 The Kashmir residency: memories of 1939 and 1940.
Evelyn Désirée Battye.   London: BACSA, 1997. 142p.

The Resident, stationed at all the major princely capitals during the colonial period, was the link between the British authorities in Delhi and the state rulers. Although for much of the time he played a largely ceremonial and representational role, he could in some cases intervene forcefully in state affairs, as happened in Kashmir during the late 19th century. The present piece is a nostalgic look back by a young woman who went to Srinagar in 1939 and 1940 as the personal assistant to the Resident, whose brother-in-law she duly marries. She writes of entertaining the Maharaja, of hunting trips and other distractions, as well as reporting the Resident's view of his job.

131 The wrongs of Cashmere: a plea for the deliverance of that beautiful country from the slavery and oppression under which it is going to ruin.
Arthur Brinckman.   London: Thomas Bosworth, 1868. 48p.

Brinckman served as a missionary in Kashmir for some years, and in this pamphlet he is highly critical both of the British for allowing Kashmir to be sold to the Dogra dynasty in the Treaty of Amritsar, and of the then Maharaja, Gulab Singh, for his exploitation and oppression of his own people. He considers Gulab Singh to be a weak man, misled by his officials. He is particularly irate over what he regards as the persecution of the small Christian minority, and the final conclusion of the pamphlet, that the British ought to revoke the treaty and annex Kashmir, seems motivated by his desire to have a more accessible field for missionary activity. In 1870, an unnamed defender of the Maharaja took Brinckman on and addressed his charges one by one in *The Maharaja of Kashmeer and his calumniators* (Tours, France: Imprimerie de J. Bouserez, 1870). Most of the pamphlet is devoted to Brinckman, but a couple of pages at the end are devoted to Robert Thorp's attack on the Maharaja (see entry no. 143).

132   Islam and political mobilization in Kashmir, 1931-34.
Ian Copland.   *Pacific Affairs*, vol. 54 (1988), p. 228-59. map.
Ian Copland's important article starts from a consideration of Mohammed Ali Jinnah's
view that all South Asia's Muslims formed a single nation, and the difficulty of applying
this to the circumstances of groups such as the Muslims of Kashmir. He approaches the
issue through an analysis of the agitation in Kashmir against the ruler in 1931-34. It was
this movement which brought Sheikh Abdullah to prominence and began to set the stage
for 1947. Copland's conclusion is that specifically religious factors did play a part in the
anti-Maharaja movement, but that it would be misleading to see them operating except in
the specific context of Kashmir's internal politics, which among other things included
sharp divisions among different Muslim groups. Copland develops his theme in relation
to the 1947 period in 'The Abdullah factor: Kashmiri Muslims and the crisis of 1947' (in
The Political inheritance of Pakistan [Edited by D. A. Low. London: Macmillan, 1991]).

133   The princes of India in the endgame of empire, 1917-1947.
Ian Copland.   Cambridge, England: Cambridge University Press,
1997. 302p. bibliog. (Cambridge Studies in Indian History and
Society 2).
Copland's *magnum opus* on the princely order in the last years of British rule includes
many specific references to Kashmir, as well as analysing the dilemmas facing the
princely order as a whole. Other general works on the Indian princes in the 20th century
are: Stephen Ashton, *British policy towards the Indian states, 1905-1939* (London:
Curzon Press, 1982); Urmila Phadnis, *Towards the integration of the Indian states*
(Bombay, India: Asia Publishing House, 1968); Barbara Ramusack, *The princes of India
in the twilight of empire: dissolution of a patron-client system, 1914-1939* (Columbus,
Ohio: Ohio State University Press, 1978).

**134   Condemned unheard: the Government of India and H. H. the
Maharaja of Kashmir.**
William Digby.   Delhi; Madras, India: Asian Educational Services,
1994. 226p.
This is a facsimile reprint of a famous pamphlet published in 1890 to put the case of
Maharaja Pratap Singh against the removal of his powers the previous year and the
imposition of a British regent in the state. The decision had been taken because of the
official view that Pratap Singh was weak and hopelessly incompetent. Digby was a
radical journalist of the time and closely associated with the early nationalist movement,
and his writing is a vigorous attack on official duplicity and high-handedness, which he
compares to the worst aspects of British rule in Ireland. A lengthy appendix reproduces
many of the relevant documents from British Parliamentary Papers and from Hansard.

**135   The making of a frontier: five years' experiences and adventures
in Gilgit, Hunza, Nagar, Chitral, and the eastern Hindu-Kush.**
Algernon Durand.   London: John Murray, 1899. 298p. map.
Durand was one of the key figures in the implementation of British frontier policy along
the north-west borders. In the present work he describes in detail the five years that he
spent from 1889 to 1894 as the first British agent at Gilgit, during which time he was able
to assert British influence in the region and bring it within the British scheme of things.

This was not always an easy undertaking, and Durand had to take on and defeat a major uprising in 1891.

136 Socialist ideas and movements in Kashmir (1919-1947).
Manzoor Fazili.   Delhi: Eureka Publications, 1980. 218p. bibliog.

Originally a PhD thesis, this book argues the case that socialist ideas have been a major force in Kashmir. It focuses especially on the National Conference led by Sheikh Abdullah, and on one of its key documents, 'Naya Kashmir' (New Kashmir), produced in 1944, which called for the right to land for the cultivator, the abolition of moneylending, and industrialization. There are also chapters on radical poetry in Urdu and Kashmiri, notably the work of Mahjoor and Abdul Ahad Azad.

137 Kashmir in transition 1885-1893.
Dilip Kumar Ghose.   Calcutta, India: World Press, 1975. 261p. map. bibliog.

This period saw the Government of India greatly increase its control of Jammu and Kashmir, first in 1885 by insisting on stationing a 'Resident' in the state, and then in 1889 by the effective supersession of the ruler by a British-appointed council (although his powers were later restored). Ghose's solid piece of imperial history brings out British concerns over Kashmir's strategic position at a time when Britain and Russia were competing for influence in Central Asia. It was also during this period that the British took direct control of the Gilgit Agency, an arrangement that lasted nearly until independence.

138 Social and economic history of Jammu and Kashmir state, 1885 to 1925 A.D.
M. L. Kapur.   Delhi: Anmol Publications, 1992. 451p. bibliog.

The title of this work is slightly misleading, as it really consists of source material for such a history, covering the rule of Maharaja Pratap Singh. The author draws on a very wide range of government reports, census publications, gazetteers and other material. He gives a detailed picture of social conditions and economic production, together with an excellent bibliography, but does not offer any broader framework of analysis.

139 Freedom struggle in Jammu and Kashmir.
Santosh Kaul.   Delhi: Anmol Publications, 1990. 209p.

A straightforward political history of Kashmir from the creation of the state of Jammu and Kashmir in 1846 up to its accession to India in October 1947. The author has based her work, which goes into considerable detail, on a wide range of published and unpublished documentary material, on newspapers, and on interviews with participants for the last phase. There is substantial coverage of the emergence of the National Conference and the role of Sheikh Abdullah.

140 Political awakening in Kashmir.
Ravinderjit Kaur.   Delhi: APH Publishing Corporation, 1996. 226p. bibliog.

Based on extensive archival research in Delhi and Srinagar, the work, originally a doctoral thesis, covers the period from the late 19th century up to the first popular movement in 1931. The author looks at the impact of Western education, the growth of middle-class social and political activism among all the state's communities, and the initial agitation to reserve jobs for 'state subjects', which in practice often meant local Muslims as opposed to Hindus, who were already overrepresented in government. Against this background she then describes the genesis of the 1931 movement, which took on a more specifically communal coloration, and in her view overwhelmed the secular character of earlier political activism.

141 Kashmir politics and imperialist manoeuvres 1846-1980.

N. N. Raina. Delhi: Patriot Publishers, 1988. 276p. bibliog.

This is a general account of Kashmir's history since the state's formation, written from a broadly Marxist perspective.

142 Kashmiris fight – for freedom. Vol. 1, 1819-1946.

Muhammad Yusuf Saraf. Lahore, Pakistan: Kashmir History Committee, 1977. 708p. map. bibliog.

The author, chief justice of the Azad Jammu and Kashmir High Court at the time the book was written, has woven together material from a wide variety of sources into a readable narrative of events. He focuses especially on the events of 1931 and the period from then to the eve of Indian independence.

143 Cashmere misgovernment.

Robert Thorp. London: Longmans, Green & Co., 1870. 80p.

Robert Thorp, whose mother was in fact Kashmiri, uses this pamphlet to accuse the Kashmiri state of systematic oppression of its subjects. One chapter is devoted to the plight of the shawl-weavers, treated as virtual serfs. Thorp calls on the British to fulfil their moral responsibility to the Kashmiri population. The pamphlet was originally published in Calcutta (Wyman Bros.) in 1868, the year of Thorp's death in Srinagar, according to some accounts in mysterious circumstances, raising the possibility of murder by the Maharaja's agents. In 1980, a reprinted version appeared – *Kashmir misgovernment*, edited and recast by F. M. Hassnain (Srinagar, India: Gulshan Publishers). However, it should be noted that although this includes Thorp's original text, it also includes a number of editorial insertions in the voice of Thorp, which cannot be easily distinguished from the original.

144 History of the freedom struggle in Jammu and Kashmir.

Edited by Mohammad Yasin and A. Qaiyum Rafiqi. Delhi: Light and Life Publishers, 1980. 256p. bibliog.

A varied and useful collection of twenty papers originally given at a seminar in 1978. Some of the authors are historians, others public figures drawing on their own recollections. The papers include general attempts at conceptual clarification as well as specific studies of women in the freedom struggle and poets such as Mahjoor. The overall thrust of the collection is to see a harmony between Kashmiri aspirations and the broader Indian struggle.

145 Emergence of political awakening in Kashmir.
U. K. Zutshi. Delhi: Manohar, 1986. 252p. map. bibliog.

The aim of this work, originally a PhD thesis, is to put into context the 1931 agitation, which launched the career of Sheikh Abdullah and is generally regarded as the starting point of modern political activity in Kashmir. The author gives most weight to the impact of British colonial policy in general and as it affected a princely state such as Jammu and Kashmir. The Muslim population were encouraged to think of themselves in communal terms and to demand greater representation in the Hindu-dominated administration of the Maharaja, and this was brought to a head in 1931. The book itself concentrates on the period preceding the agitation and not the confrontation itself.

Partition and disputed accession

146 The emergence of Pakistan.
Chaudhri Muhammad Ali. New York, London: Columbia University Press, 1967. 418p. maps.

Chaudhri Muhammad Ali, who became Prime Minister of Pakistan in the mid-1950s, was a senior civil servant at the time of independence and became Pakistan's representative on the steering committee of the Partition Council. This carefully written memoir, which depends on written sources as well as the author's own recollections, deals with the situation immediately before and after 15 August 1947. He has some interesting accounts of meetings with Indian National Congress leaders Jawaharlal Nehru and Vallabhbhai Patel, and suggests that the latter might well have been prepared to offer a deal involving Kashmir and Hyderabad at an early stage.

147 Captive Kashmir.
Aziz Beg. Lahore, Pakistan: Allied Business Corporation, 1957. 202p.

An uncompromising statement of the Pakistani position on the accession and subsequent history of Kashmir up to the time of writing, and a bitter attack on Indian motives and actions. There is an extensive appendix that provides numerous quotes from foreign newspapers supporting the Pakistani position. The book has a foreword by the then President of Azad Kashmir, Sardar Mohammad Ibrahim Khan.

148 Halfway to freedom.
Margaret Bourke-White. New York: Simon & Schuster, 1949. 245p. map.

The famous American photographer visited India and Pakistan just after independence. This personal memoir includes an eyewitness account of the early stages of the fighting in late 1947. Her assessment of Sheikh Abdullah and his colleagues is very positive, while she is critical of Pakistan's role. The book contains a number of her photographs, a couple of which relate to Kashmir.

149 Thunder over Kashmir.
Maurice Cohen. Hyderabad, India: Orient Longman, 1994. 116p. map.

Originally published in 1955, this book claims to be the first eyewitness account of the 1947-48 war by a soldier on the Indian side. Cohen, who belonged to the small Indian Jewish community, describes in particular the defence and subsequent relief of Poonch city, in which he took part from April 1948 onwards. The book is illustrated with some rather grainy black-and-white photographs.

150 Mountbatten and independent India.
Larry Collins, Dominique Lapierre. Delhi: Vikas, 1984. 193p.

Collins and Lapierre were the authors of the at times rather highly coloured account of independence and partition, *Freedom at midnight* (London: Collins, 1975). This present volume reproduces the texts of the interviews they conducted with Lord Mountbatten as part of the research for that book, together with a number of documents written by or for Mountbatten during his time as Viceroy. The Kashmir issue features prominently in both sections. Mountbatten is quoted as saying that he had initially wanted Kashmir to go to Pakistan, following the Hindu-Muslim logic of the partition plan as a whole, and blaming Maharaja Hari Singh's hesitation for the subsequent debacle.

151 Sardar Patel's correspondence 1945-50. Volume 1. New Light on Kashmir.
Edited by Durga Das. Ahmedabad, India: Navajivan Publishing House, 1971. 394p.

Vallabhbhai Patel, often known by his honorific title of Sardar, was one of the most prominent nationalist leaders in India and became deputy Prime Minister from 1947 until his death in 1950. He was also formally in charge of the integration of the princely states into the Indian Union. Patel is usually identified as the conservative voice of Indian nationalist politics. Whereas Nehru found a natural affinity with Sheikh Abdullah, Patel was more sympathetic to the plight of the Maharaja (Prem Shankar Jha uses this tension to explain the inconsistencies in the historical record relating to the accession [see entry no. 155]). The present volume contains a large number of letters relating to Kashmir, some of minor importance but others of considerable significance, for example Patel's correspondence with Ramchandra Kak, the state's Prime Minister until September 1947. Recent biographies of Patel which touch on Kashmir include Rani Dhavan Shankardass, *Vallabhbhai Patel: power and organization in Indian politics* (London: Sangam Books; Hyderabad, India: Orient Longman, 1988) and Rajmohan Gandhi, *Patel: a life* (Ahmedabad, India: Navajivan Publishing House, 1991).

152 Liberty or death: India's journey to independence and division.
Patrick French. London: HarperCollins, 1997. 467p. maps. bibliog.

This is the most up-to-date of the more popular accounts of Indian independence, and is written with the advantage of access to the British Indian government's secret intelligence files, now available to researchers. There is a section on the Kashmir issue, framed by the author's general view that Britain withdrew from India because by 1947 it had effectively lost control of the situation. An earlier general account of partition which also covers the Kashmir issue is *The last days of the British Raj*, by Leonard Mosley (London:

Weidenfeld & Nicholson, 1961). Mosley believes that the British could and should have taken more time in realizing the hand-over of power.

153 The great divide: Britain – India – Pakistan.

H. V. Hodson.   Karachi, Pakistan: Oxford University Press, 1985.
2nd ed. 590p. bibliog.

Although originally published in 1969 without access to all the documentation that subsequently became available, this book is valuable both because of its considerable merits as a literary work and because its author had free access to the papers of Lord Mountbatten, the last viceroy. Mountbatten is very much the central figure and Hodson rates his achievements very highly. A separate chapter is devoted to 'Conflict in Kashmir', which begins with Mountbatten's visit to Kashmir from 18-23 June 1947 and covers his efforts to bring about a peaceful solution once the conflict had started.

154 Kashmir dispute: an international law perspective.

Ijaz Hussain.   Islamabad, Pakistan: Quaid-i-Azam University,
National Institute of Pakistan Studies, Quaid-i-Azam Chair, 1998.
309p. bibliog.

Writing as an international lawyer, the author details and defends Pakistan's position on a number of issues relating to the Kashmir dispute, for example the state's status as a disputed territory, the application of the principle of self-determination, and the relevance of the UN Resolutions on Kashmir. Fourteen key documents are included as appendices. An earlier work by the same author, *Issues in Pakistan's foreign policy: an international law perspective* (Lahore, Pakistan: Progressive Publishers, 1988) includes an article on the Wullar Barrage project, a dam which India would like to construct in its part of Kashmir and to which Pakistan objects.

155 Kashmir, 1947: rival versions of history.

Prem Shankar Jha.   Delhi: Oxford University Press, 1996. 151p.

This work by a senior Indian journalist and writer is an extended review and critique of the work of Alastair Lamb (see entry no. 159). He tackles head-on Lamb's claims about the collusion between Mountbatten and the Indian government in 1947 to deprive Pakistan of Kashmir. Even if Jha does not manage to rebut these claims totally, he does provide a plausible alternative reading of some of the key issues that Lamb raises. Two in particular are subject to careful scrutiny. The first is the question of whether the line of partition drawn by Lord Radcliffe in August 1947 was altered at Mountbatten's behest to allow India a land route into Kashmir. The second relates to whether the instrument of accession was signed before or after the first Indian troops landed in Srinagar on 27 October 1947. Jha accepts Lamb's contention that it could not have been signed on the 26 October, as claimed in the published accounts, but argues that it was signed on 25 October and not after the event. He suggests that the reason for this was a struggle between Jawaharlal Nehru and Vallabhbhai Patel over how the state should be absorbed into India. Jha also discusses some of the broader issues to do with the state of communal relations in Kashmir in 1947 and the geopolitical framework within which decisions were made.

156 Kashmir on trial: State versus Sheikh Abdullah.
Lahore: Lion Press, 1947. 224p.

This book contains Sheikh Abdullah's address to the court that was trying him in 1946 on charges of seditious speeches, and the submission by his defence counsel, the leading Indian nationalist lawyer, Asaf Ali. The issue at stake was Sheikh Abdullah's right to speak out for the Kashmiri people's right to have responsible government. There is an introduction by Jawaharlal Nehru, who was deeply concerned about the fate of the popular movement in Kashmir.

157 Raiders in Kashmir.
Akbar Khan.   Islamabad, Pakistan: National Book Foundation, 1975. 2nd ed. 210p. map.

First published in 1970, this work caused something of a stir, as it set out in detail how the Pakistani army, under instructions from the government, had organized the incursion into Kashmir of armed tribesmen from the North-West Frontier Province, something that had not been admitted at the time. The author, a very senior officer on the Pakistani side who, under the *nom-de-guerre* of General Tariq, was responsible for the organization of the incursion, gives a detailed account of subsequent fighting. Akbar Khan later became involved in the Rawalpindi Conspiracy in 1951 (in which fifteen officers of the Pakistani army plotted to overthrow the civilian government), and the book also contains his version of these events.

158 Danger in Kashmir.
Josef Korbel.   Princeton, New Jersey: Princeton University Press, 1954. 351p. maps. bibliog.

An early but still valuable account of the Kashmir dispute by a member of the UN commission which tried in the early stages to bring about an agreed solution. Korbel describes the background and origins of the dispute and then goes into detail on the work of the UN and its representatives. Appendices include relevant UN documents.

159 Incomplete partition: the genesis of the Kashmir dispute.
Alastair Lamb.   Hertingfordbury, England: Roxford Books, 1997. 374p. maps.

This book is best seen as an appendix to the author's *Kashmir: a disputed legacy 1846-1990* (see entry no. 87). In it he fills out the story as he sees it of events from the arrival of the last Viceroy, Lord Mountbatten, until the end of the initial fighting in late 1948. Written with meticulous attention to detail, and based on the mass of documentation about the high politics of partition that has become available over the past couple of decades, Lamb casts doubt on several key elements of the standard accounts, including, most famously, the question of whether the Maharaja signed the instrument of accession on 26 October, or, as he suggests, the following day and thus after the first Indian troops had reached Srinagar, or even not at all (the actual instrument of accession has never been found). In the view of Pakistan, if the accession was signed only after the event, then the whole basis of India's claim that the accession is legal falls. The book's claims have been vigorously refuted by Prem Shankar Jha (see entry no. 155). Lamb's conclusions can be found in a preliminary form in *Birth of a tragedy: Kashmir 1947* (Hertingfordbury, England: Roxford Books, 1994).

160 Constitutional relations between Britain and India: the transfer of power 1942-7.
Editor-in-Chief, Nicholas Mansergh; editors and assistant editors, E. W. R. Lumby (vols. 1-4) and Penderel Moon (vols. 5-12). London: Her Majesty's Stationery Office, 1970-83. 12 vols. maps.

This truly monumental project is on a scale never likely to be repeated in the field of South Asian studies. The twelve volumes, each around 900 pages and impeccably edited, contain all the documents of any significance from the British archives that bear on the question of how and why policy was framed as it was. From the telegrams, minutes, notes, etc. that are included, it is possible to build up an immensely rich and detailed picture of the progress of events on the British side. Even though a complete story would require equal documentation from Congress and Muslim League leaders, something which does not exist (although on the Pakistani side a scholarly edition of some of the Jinnah papers is under preparation – see entry no. 168), by itself the *Transfer of Power* series is an invaluable source for any serious scholar of the subject. The series finishes with the formal transfer of power on 15 August 1947, so the crisis over Kashmir is not covered, but there are significant references to developments in the state in most of the volumes. The private diary of Lord Wavell (*The Viceroy's journal*, edited by Penderel Moon [London: Oxford University Press, 1973]), who held office as viceroy from 1943 until the arrival of Mountbatten in March 1947, also contains some interesting insights.

161 The story of the integration of the Indian states.
V. P. Menon. Bombay, India: Orient Longmans, 1956. 489p. maps

Menon was the man who made the dramatic (and now disputed – see the debate between Lamb and Jha [entry nos. 155 and 159]) visits to Srinagar on 25 October and to Jammu the following day which led to the Maharaja signing the instrument of accession. He was also the key official adviser to Sardar Vallabhbhai Patel in negotiations with the Indian princely states. He wrote his own account of the period in two volumes (the period up to 15 August 1947 is covered in *The transfer of power in India* [Bombay, India: Orient Longmans, 1957]). A chapter is devoted to the Kashmir situation, and he gives a graphic account, often quoted by later writers, of the atmosphere in Srinagar as the tribal invaders approached and the Maharaja realized that he had no choice but to accede to India. Another account, this time by a British official who went on to help edit the *Transfer of power* volumes (see entry no. 160), is by E. W. R. Lumby, *The transfer of power in India, 1945-7* (London: George Allen & Unwin, 1954).

162 Making the new Commonwealth.
Robin J. Moore. Oxford: Clarendon Press, 1987. 218p. bibliog.

This is an account of the 'high politics' involved in finding ways in which the newly independent states of South Asia could be included in what had till then been restricted to Britain and the white dominions. The Kashmir issue and the war of 1947-48 form a significant part of the story, in that a settlement could not be reached until peace had been restored between India and Pakistan, both of which did eventually join the British Commonwealth as it emerged from the Commonwealth Conference in April 1949.

163 The partition of India: policies and perspectives 1935-1947.
Edited by C. H. Philips, Mary Doreen Wainwright. London:
George Allen & Unwin, 1970. 607p. bibliog.

The valuable papers included in this volume were originally presented to a conference in London in 1967 which brought together Pakistani, Indian and British participants in the events of 1947 as well as scholars from the three countries. Thirteen papers, mainly but not exclusively by academics, are included in the first section on policies and parties, including a piece by E. W. R. Lumby on the princely states, and sixteen in the second on perspectives and reflections. Kashmir is not the focus of attention in any of the contributions, but there are a number of references to the situation there, and the volume as a whole makes very useful background reading.

164 Armed forces of the Indian Union: history of operations in Jammu & Kashmir (1947-48).
S. N. Prasad, Dharm Pal. Delhi: Government of India, Ministry of Defence, Historical Division, 1987. 418p. maps. bibliog.

A detailed, almost entirely military account of the 1947-1948 war. Each unit's role in the fighting is described, as well as individual acts of valour. Appendices include the United Nations document recording the delimitation of the cease-fire line in July 1949.

165 Selected works of Jawaharlal Nehru.
Delhi: Orient Longman, 1972-78. 11 vols. (1st Series); Delhi:
Jawaharlal Nehru Memorial Fund (distributed by Oxford University Press), 1984- . (2nd Series)

The *Selected works* of Nehru form a major source for any academic study of the Kashmir issue. They include all of Nehru's major speeches and writings, a large part of his private correspondence and a few items from government records. The first series goes up to 1940, while the second starts from September 1946, when Nehru became deeply involved in the negotiations leading to the transfer of power. The documents printed show the deep interest he took in all aspects of the Kashmir question. An additional source for Nehru's views on Kashmir are his published letters to the chief ministers of the Indian states (provinces), which he sent frequently from 1947 until his death in 1964 (*Letters to Chief Ministers 1947-1964* [Delhi: Jawaharlal Memorial Fund, distributed by Oxford University Press, 1985-89. 5 vols.]). He often used these letters to keep his colleagues up to date on negotiations and to offer his own views.

166 Slender was the thread: Kashmir confrontation, 1947-48.
L. P. Sen. Delhi: Orient Longmans, 1969. 308p. maps.

The author was commander of the 161 Infantry Brigade, which was involved throughout the fighting in 1947-48, first with the 'tribal raiders' and then with units of the regular Pakistani army. Much of the book is a detailed and first-hand account of military operations, written in an approachable style. There are also sections in which the author writes of the broader picture at the time.

167 **Without baggage: a personal account of the Jammu & Kashmir operations October 1947-January 1949.**
E. A. Vas.   Dehradun, India: Natraj Publishers, 1987. 173p. map.

As a young officer, the author served in the war with Pakistan that followed Kashmir's accession to India and was present on the ground from early November 1947. After an initial chapter devoted largely to the political background, General Vas intermingles recollections of the fighting with reflections on how mountain warfare should be conducted.

168 **Quaid-i-Azam Mohammad Ali Jinnah papers.**
Edited by Z. H. Zaidi.   Islamabad, Pakistan: National Archives of Pakistan, 1993- .

This major publishing project, which will occupy many volumes when eventually complete, is intended to be a counterpart to the *Transfer of power* series (see entry no. 160) and thus a major source for the history of the period, including the dispute over Kashmir. Once complete, it will include all the available letters to and from Jinnah, as well as other relevant material. There are many references to Kashmir affairs and to the strategies being pursued by the various parties. The format of each volume follows that of the *Transfer of power* series, with an introduction setting out the events of the period covered, explanatory notes to each document, and indices of persons and subjects.

Post-1948

169 **Modern history of Jammu and Kashmir: a look back into ancient glorious Kashmir focusing confrontation and failures leading to present turbulent Kashmir and a peep ahead. (Including select documents and comprehensive reference bibliography covering all aspects of Jammu and Kashmir, 1844-1994).**
J. C. Aggarwal, S. P. Agrawal.   Delhi: Concept Publishing Company, 1995. 2 vols. 807p. (continuous pagination). bibliog.

Despite the title, this is in fact almost entirely a collection of documents from 1947 to the early 1990s. The first volume covers the period up to the Simla Agreement of 1972, and the second goes up to 1994. There is substantial coverage of United Nations Security Council resolutions and speeches from all concerned. The work also includes the texts of key agreements, for example between Mrs Gandhi and Sheikh Abdullah in 1975. The reference bibliography at the end of the second volume lists some 3,000 items, the majority of which are items from Indian newspapers and journals, but many books are also included.

170   Kashmir in crucible.
Prem Nath Bazaz.   Delhi: Pamposh Publications, 1967. 318p.
As well as an established commentator on Kashmir affairs, Bazaz was a political activist working for an agreed solution to the problem, and the present work is a critique of official policy towards the state after the arrest of Sheikh Abdullah in 1953. He discusses the implications of the 1965 war, and calls for a secular solution based on an Indian willingness to allow a substantial degree of autonomy to the state. An appendix gives the text of his correspondence with Nehru, both before and after 1947. An earlier work by Bazaz along similar lines, but with an extensive section covering the pre-1947 period, is *The history of struggle for freedom in Kashmir, cultural and political, from the earliest times to the present day* (Delhi: Kashmir Publishing Company, 1954).

171   Two nations and Kashmir.
Christopher [Lord] Birdwood.   London: Robert Hale, 1956. 237p. maps.
A frequently cited analysis of the Kashmir issue written in the 1950s by a retired Indian army officer. Birdwood reviews the events of 1947 and the subsequent efforts to hold a plebiscite. Like many others, he suggests a solution that envisages the partition of the state following a series of regional plebiscites.

172   The struggle for Kashmir.
Michael Brecher.   New York: Oxford University Press, 1953. 211p. bibliog.
Michael Brecher, best known for his major biography of Jawaharlal Nehru, published this general study of the Kashmir problem after interviews and fieldwork in India and Pakistan in 1951-52. He highlights the negative consequences of the dispute for both countries. Much of the work is devoted to the UN's mediation efforts that were made during the early years after 1947 (see also Brecher's article, 'Kashmir: a case study in United Nations mediation', *Pacific Affairs*, vol. 26, no. 3 [September 1953], p. 195-207).

173   India decides: elections 1952-1995.
David Butler, Ashok Lahiri, Prannoy Roy.   Delhi: Books & Things, 1995. 405p. maps.
A reliable compendium of the constituency-level results in successive national elections by three leading psephologists. Elections to the state legislature (the Vidhan Sabha) for the 1962-83 period are covered by V. B. Singh and Shankar Bose in *State elections in India: data handbook on Vidhan Sabha elections 1952-85* (Delhi: Sage Publications, 1987).

174   Genesis of regional conflicts: Kashmir, Afghanistan, West Asia, Cambodia, Chechnya.
Edited by V. D. Chopra, M. Rasgotra.   Delhi: Gyan Publishing House, 1995. 316p.
The focus of this collection, edited by a well-known journalist (Chopra) and a retired head of India's diplomatic service (Rasgotra), is the genesis of regional conflicts in the post-cold-war period. Kashmir is the subject of the largest number of articles, many of which are in fact written by V. D. Chopra. He and several of the other contributors are sharply

critical of both Pakistan and the United States, and their analysis of the rise of militancy links it very much to interference from across the line of control, although Rasgotra's introduction includes some critical remarks on the way the Indian government handled Kashmir affairs in the 1980s. The chapter by B. K. Srivastava looks in detail at the US position on Kashmir during the first term of the Clinton administration.

175 The peacekeepers of Kashmir: the UN Military Observer Group in India and Pakistan.
Pauline Dawson.   London: Hurst; New York: St. Martin's Press, 1994. 337p. bibliog.

The Military Observer Group (UNMOGIP) was set up by the UN in 1949 to monitor the cease-fire line established at the beginning of the year. Its role has gradually been pared down over the years, and since 1972 it has no longer been allowed to operate on the Indian side of the line. However, Pauline Dawson's detailed study, based on UN documents and files and originally a PhD thesis, makes the case that it contributed significantly to the maintenance of peace between India and Pakistan in the period up to the 1971 war, despite the 1965 conflict. Since then, she suggests that UNMOGIP's role has been mainly symbolic, although under certain circumstances its operational role could be reactivated.

176 Foreign relations of the United States.
Washington: Government Printing Office.

Published by the US State Department's Bureau of Public Affairs, this long-running series includes the texts of many major documents, including correspondence from US ambassadors in the field and internal discussion documents and memoranda. Private at the time, they have now been put into the public domain in accordance with official policy. Although items that are regarded as still sensitive are excluded, there is still a huge amount of primary material to be found, and historians have often made good use of it. The volumes that cover South Asia have a great deal of information on US positions towards the Kashmir conflict. There is no standard periodicity or pattern to the volumes and they appear from fifteen to thirty years after the events they describe. The latest edition covers the 1965 Indo-Pakistan war.

177 Ambassador's journal: a personal account of the Kennedy years.
John Kenneth Galbraith.   London: Hamish Hamilton, 1969. 656p.

Galbraith, equally famous as an economist, was Kennedy's ambassador to India and a high-profile figure who got on well with his Indian hosts. His journal contains accounts of his own visits to Kashmir, and notes about his ring-side view of the US-British efforts to solve the Kashmir question in the aftermath of the Indo-China war (and his own occasional interventions).

178 Ayub Khan: Pakistan's first military ruler.
Altaf Gauhar.   Lahore, Pakistan: Sang-e-Meel Publications, 1993. 540p.

Altaf Gauhar was a senior civil servant during Ayub Khan's period of power in Pakistan from 1958 to 1969, and is often regarded as his *éminence grise*. This study is closely based on his own participation in the events described. Two chapters are devoted to the Kashmir issue, and there is a detailed account of the formulation and implementation of

'Operation Gibraltar', the scheme to infiltrate Pakistani soldiers into Kashmir in order to incite a popular uprising, which in turn would lead to decisive Pakistani intervention. In the end, no popular rising occurred and the Indo-Pakistan war that followed ended in stalemate. Gauhar's account is very critical of the adventurist role he believes was played by Z. A. Bhutto, at that time Pakistan's foreign minister, and by other senior military and civilian officials. Gauhar was also closely associated with the preparation of Ayub Khan's autobiography (*Friends not masters: a political autobiography* [London: Oxford University Press, 1967]). This stops short of the 1965 war, but has an account of the talks with India on the Kashmir issue at the end of 1962.

179 With great truth and respect.
Paul Gore-Booth.   London: Constable, 1974. 440p.

Lord Gore-Booth, who finished his career as head of the British diplomatic service, was Britain's High Commissioner in India from 1960 to 1965. During this period he was involved in the diplomatic efforts by Britain and the US to bring about a negotiated settlement of the Kashmir issue between Jawaharlal Nehru and Ayub Khan. He gives a brief but succinct account of these efforts in late 1962 and again in May 1963, and explains why a settlement could not be achieved. It should be read in conjunction with Galbraith (see entry no. 177).

180 Vengeance: India after the assassination of Indira Gandhi.
Pranay Gupte.   New York, London: W. W. Norton, 1985. 368p. bibliog.

Written in a personal style by a *New York Times* journalist of Indian origin, this is an account of India in the period of political upheaval following the assassination of Indira Gandhi in October 1984. The thirty-four pages on Kashmir blend historical material with interviews with leading figures such as the Mirwaiz (the most revered religious leader of the Valley), Maulvi Muhammad Farooq, assassinated in 1990.

181 The Kashmir question.
Edited by K. Sarwar Hasan.   Karachi, Pakistan: Pakistan Institute of International Affairs, 1966. 484p. (Documents on the Foreign Relations of Pakistan).

Intended as a source book, this volume brings together without commentary key documents from Pakistani and Indian sources as well as from the United Nations. While all the documents are available elsewhere, this is a useful compendium.

182 Kashmir: a tale of shame.
Hari Jaisingh.   Delhi: UBSPD, 1996. 235p. bibliog.

In many ways, this book, written without polemic, represents mainstream Indian public opinion on the subject of Kashmir. The author is a prominent journalist, and his work surveys Kashmiri history, especially since 1947, in order to show that the state is an integral part of India and will only flourish once it is properly integrated with the rest of the country. He is especially critical of the role played by Sheikh Abdullah. He does, however, argue that the dispute with Pakistan could be settled by changing the line of control into an international boundary. Internally, he argues for a strict security regime, alongside the revival of political activity based on the electoral process.

183 The Kashmir tangle: issues and options.
Rajesh Kadian. Boulder, Colorado: Westview Press; Lahore, Pakistan: Pak Book Corporation; Delhi: Vision Books, 1993. 205p. maps. bibliog.

A general overview which aims at a detached analysis of the situation in Kashmir, mainly from 1947 on, and which is critical of all parties to the conflict. Kadian is particularly interested in the military and strategic dimensions. The final chapter discusses the options available to India and Pakistan, although he comes to pessimistic conclusions about the likelihood of any agreed solution emerging.

184 Kashmir: problems and politics.
B. L. Kak. Delhi: Seema Publications, 1981. 173p. bibliog.

This book was written to make the point that foreign powers, the US in particular but also the Soviet Union and China, are interested in imposing solutions to the Kashmir dispute that would serve their own interests in the region. The author discusses the activities of the US ambassador to India in 1950, and sees a direct link with a visit to Kashmir in 1978 by Governor Nelson Rockefeller.

185 Kashmir: convictions betrayed. Legacies of Abdullah-Nehru nexus.
O. P. Kapoor. Chandigarh, India: Arun Publishing House, 1995. 160p.

As the title suggests, this is a polemic that traces the 1989 uprising to the malign intentions of Sheikh Abdullah and the support he received from Nehru. The former is portrayed as first and foremost a communal Muslim, and also as corrupt and power-hungry. In addition, the book includes material on the difficulties faced by the Pandit community since 1989.

186 Crisis in Kashmir.
Pyarelal Kaul. Srinagar, India; Delhi: Suman Publications, 1991. 330p.

A personal view of Kashmiri politics by someone who has been active in various political parties over many years. He is critical of the actions of both Nehru and Sheikh Abdullah, and clearly identifies with the interests of his own Pandit community. A second volume by Kaul, *Kashmir: trail* (sic) *and travail* (Srinagar, India; Delhi: Suman Publications, 1996) pursues similar themes and focuses more specifically on the difficulties faced by the Pandits who fled Kashmir in the early 1990s and have remained as internal refugees since then.

187 Kashmir and the United Nations.
Rahmatullah Khan. Delhi: Vikas Publications, 1969. 199p. bibliog.

A detailed analysis by an Indian international lawyer of the United Nation's involvement in the Kashmir question, with particular reference to the discussions at the time of the 1965 Indo-Pakistan war. In the author's view, the UN has misconstrued its role as being to attempt to resolve the basic dispute. It should instead, he argues, have confined itself to dealing with the original armed provocation from Pakistani territory.

188 My years with Nehru: Kashmir.
B. N. Mullik.   Bombay, India: Allied, 1971.

B. N. Mullik was head of the Intelligence Bureau for most of Nehru's period as Prime Minister, and one of his closest advisers. As might be expected from an intelligence officer, he places much of the blame for the problems in Kashmir on the machinations of the Pakistani intelligence services. The centrepiece of the book is the conspiracy case brought in 1962-64 against Sheikh Abdullah, of whom Mullik is very critical. The book includes facsimile copies of many of the documents and letters seized by Indian intelligence agents from Pakistani infiltrators.

189 The Kashmir question.
A. G. Noorani.   Bombay, India: Manaktalas, 1964. 125p.

A remarkably balanced analysis of the position in Jammu and Kashmir, written at a key moment in the 1960s just after the release of Sheikh Abdullah. The author, a well-known constitutional lawyer, takes the view that 'while Kashmir's accession to India is perfectly legal and valid, it is provisional'. This means, he says, that there is still room for a compromise based on negotiations involving the people of Kashmir as well as the governments of India and Pakistan. The book is valuable both for its own suggestions and for its succinct account of negotiations between India and Pakistan and the role of the United Nations.

190 Simmering volcano: study of Jammu's relations with Kashmir.
Balraj Puri.   Delhi: Sterling Publishers, 1983. 144p. bibliog.

Balraj Puri is a political commentator who has believed for many years that Jammu, which contains nearly half the population of the state of Jammu and Kashmir, has been neglected by most analysts, and that in fact a balanced relationship between Jammu and the rest of the state, based on regional autonomy, would facilitate a solution to the broader question of finding an equitable relationship between the state and the rest of India. The present work reviews the history of the state since 1947, with particular reference to the author's own role.

191 Elections and state politics of India (a case-study of Kashmir).
Zaheer Masood Quraishi.   Delhi: Sundeep Prakashan, 1979. 256p. bibliog.

This is an empirical, questionnaire-based study of the Jammu and Kashmir state elections of 1972. The areas selected for the study fell entirely in the Kashmir region. The author rejects the view that the elections were unfair to any significant extent, and sees the results as showing that the Kashmiri voter shares the same concerns as elsewhere in India.

192 Divided Kashmir: old problems, new opportunities for India, Pakistan, and the Kashmiri people.
Mushtaqur Rahman.   Boulder, Colorado; London: Lynne Rienner Publishers, 1996. 218p. maps. bibliog.

The author of this overview of the Kashmir issue is a Pakistani geographer working in the United States. The main part of the book is a historical account of the Kashmir issue since 1947, from a generally Pakistani perspective. His discussion of possible solutions to the crisis draws on the success of the Indus Waters treaty of 1960, although it should be noted that his proposed division of the state according to river basin boundaries would require the transfer of the Srinagar valley to Pakistan.

193 How Moscow sees Kashmir.
Hemen Ray.   Bombay, India: Jaico Publishing House, 1985. 150p. bibliog.

An overview of the subject based on Russian- and English-language newspaper reports. Appendices give key statements by Soviet diplomats and ministers.

194 Zulfikar Ali Bhutto and Pakistan, 1967-1977.
Rafi Raza.   Karachi, Pakistan: Oxford University Press, 1997. 403p.

The author is a lawyer who was closely associated with Mr Bhutto from early in the latter's political career, and who served as his advisor at key moments, including the negotiation of the Simla agreement in July 1972. He gives a detailed account of the minute-by-minute negotiations of the clause in the agreement that converted the cease-fire line in Kashmir into the present line of control.

195 Krishna Menon on Kashmir: speeches at the United Nations.
Edited by E. S. Reddy, A. K. Damodaran.   Delhi: Samchar Publishing House, 1992. 547p.

The major part of this work is the reprint of Krishna Menon's famous speech to the UN Security Council in January 1957 in which he set out very clearly and robustly the Indian position over the status of Jammu and Kashmir. Later speeches in 1957 and 1962 are also included. Another source for the speeches is S. R. Bakshi, *V. K. Krishna Menon: India and the Kashmir problem* (Delhi: Anmol Publications, 1994 [Indian Freedom Fighters Series 51]). The January 1957 speech is also reprinted in *V. K. Krishna Menon's marathon speech on Kashmir at the U.N. Security Council* (Allahabad, India: Wheeler Publishing, 1992), with an introduction by retired senior Indian diplomat T. N. Kaul, who was himself involved in many of the diplomatic manoeuvres over Kashmir, and appendices which give the texts of the 1947 instrument of accession and the Simla Accord (which is also reprinted by Bakshi).

196 The saga of Ladakh: heroic battles of Rezang La and Gurung Hill, 1961-62.
Jagjit Singh.   Delhi: Vanity Books, 1983. 155p.

A soldier's account, illustrated with photographs, of battles during the Sino-Indian conflict of 1962, in which Ladakh was one of the main theatres. The author was brigade major of one of the main Indian formations involved in the fighting.

197 Kashmir: behind the white curtain 1972-1991.
Khem Lata Wakhlu, O. N. Wakhlu.   Delhi: Konark Publishers, 1992. 402p.

Khem Lata Wakhlu, the principal author, was Minister of Tourism in the Jammu and Kashmir government in the mid-1980s. She and her husband, O. N. Wakhlu, were also kidnapped by militants in 1992 and released only after an army operation. The present book, most of it based on Mrs Wakhlu's personal involvement, is an attempt to describe the political events from 1972 that led to the outbreak of militancy in 1989. Although the personal detail sometimes obscures the main narrative, this is a very valuable document for any student of the period. An epilogue gives a brief but graphic account of the forty-five days that the authors spent in captivity.

198   White paper on the Jammu and Kashmir dispute.
Islamabad: Government of Pakistan, Ministry of Foreign Affairs, 1977. 137p. maps.
Concentrating mainly on the period after 1947, this Bhutto-initiated document represents the Pakistani position in the mid-1970s.

199   The rise and fall of democracy in Jammu and Kashmir.
Sten Widmalm.   *Asian Survey*, vol. 37, no. 11 (November 1997), p. 1,005-30.
A careful and detailed account of the political situation in Indian Kashmir in the years immediately preceding the 1989 uprising. Widmalm tracks in detail the breakdown of the partnership between the Congress and the National Conference led by Farooq Abdullah in 1984, and then the disputed 1987 elections. He insists that the political dimension of the situation is of central importance, and that what happened after 1989 is not necessarily a good guide to what initiated the situation. Widmalm's published PhD thesis (*Democracy and violent separatism in India: Kashmir in a comparative perspective* [Uppsala, Sweden: Uppsala University, 1997]) sets out the argument in more detail and provides useful comparisons with other parts of India.

Present crisis

200   State, nation and ethnicity in contemporary South Asia.
Ishtiaq Ahmed.   London, New York: Pinter, 1996. 326p. bibliog.
Kashmir is one of the case studies in this comparative study of ethnic political movements in South Asia. Ahmed emphasizes the economic and political roots of the present crisis, and sees Kashmiri nationalism as a subjective feeling that has developed only recently. A book with similar scope is Maya Chadda, *Ethnicity, security and separatism in India* (Delhi: Oxford University Press, 1997).

201   Terror in Indian held Kashmir: massive violation of human rights.
Shaheen Akhtar.   Islamabad: Institute of Regional Studies, 1993. 177p. (South Asian Studies IV).
The Institute of Regional Studies is a semi-official institution in Pakistan, and this report reproduces the official position, according to which India is in illegal occupation. As well as listing incidents of illegal killing etc., it also reviews the broader legal and constitutional position.

202 Mass resistance in Kashmir: origins, evolution, options.
Tahir Amin.   Islamabad: Institute of Policy Studies; Leicester,
England: The Islamic Foundation, 1995. 173p. maps. bibliog.

A Pakistani academic's view of the crisis since 1989. Amin argues that the crisis was
essentially a response to misplaced Indian policies, and therefore not the result of
Pakistani interference. He calls for continued international pressure on India to achieve a
just solution based on the wishes of the Kashmiri people, although he clearly believes that
this would lead to the state's accession to Pakistan.

203 The human rights crisis in Kashmir: a pattern of impunity.
Asia Watch, Physicians for Human Rights.   New York: Human
Rights Watch, 1993. 214p.

The 1990s crisis in Kashmir has attracted a great deal of attention from human rights
groups in the West. The two groups responsible for this report have been particularly
active, and in 1990 and 1992 sent members to Kashmir to collect evidence from victims
and eyewitnesses. The present report gives detailed accounts of extrajudicial executions,
reprisal attacks and rapes by members of the security forces. It also includes a section on
abuses committed by members of militant groups and a response by the Indian
government that criticizes both the tone and the methodology of the report as well as
rejecting specific criticisms. A report of the earlier visit was issued by the same group as
Human rights in India: Kashmir under siege (1991). Amnesty International published its
own report at about the same time: *'An unnatural fate': 'disappearances' and impunity
in the Indian states of Jammu and Kashmir and Punjab* (New York, 1993).

204 On the border of fascism: manafacture (sic) of consent in *Roja*.
Rustom Bharucha.   *Economic and Political Weekly*, vol. 29, no. 23
(4 June 1994), p. 1,389-95.

The film *Roja*, made by Mani Ratnam in 1992, was a huge popular success. A love story
set against the background of the insurgency, the militants are portrayed in highly
unflattering ways, while the hero and eponymous heroine are seen as embodiments of
Indian unity and determination to win. Bharucha's article represents a left-wing critique,
which sees the film as manufacturing an 'Indian' identity which steamrollers minority or
regional groups into conformity. An earlier article in the same journal (Tejaswini
Niranjana, 'Integrating whose nation? Tourists and terrorists in *Roja*', vol. 29, no. 3 [15
January 1994]) makes similar points.

205 Kashmir: the wounded valley.
Ajit Bhattacharjea.   Delhi: UBSPD, 1994. 312p. bibliog.

Bhattacharjea is an Indian journalist who takes a very sympathetic view of the dilemmas
facing the people of Kashmir. He provides a general overview of the background and the
present situation.

206 The challenge in Kashmir: democracy, self-determination and a just peace.

Sumantra Bose.   Delhi; Thousand Oaks, California; London: Sage Publications, 1997. 211p. bibliog.

An offshoot of the author's academic work on the links between self-determination and democracy, this is a powerful plea for the Kashmiris themselves to be allowed to settle their internal affairs. Bose argues that the present situation has been created by the systematic denial of democracy to the region both by India and by Pakistan, and that only a new dialogue in which all sides participate and which is able to explore novel solutions can produce a just settlement. The work is based on visits to Kashmir in 1995 and 1996. The latter visit coincided with the state elections in September, and Bose considers their possible contribution to a solution.

207 Regional geopolitics in a globalising world: Kashmir in geopolitical perspective.

Robert W. Bradnock.   *Geopolitics*, vol. 3, no. 1 (Autumn 1998), p. 1-29.

The author uses contemporary geopolitical theory to review the reasons why the Kashmir dispute has remained intractable. India and Pakistan, he argues, are committed to a conventional concept of statehood as equalling control over territory, but apply wholly different criteria in determining that territory's extent. He believes that this is likely to remain the case for some time to come, despite trends towards globalization, although these same trends will reawaken international interest in the Kashmir issue.

208 Kashmir imbroglio: diagnosis and remedy.

M. G. Chitkara.   Delhi: APH Publishing Corporation, 1996. 304p. bibliog.

The author, an Indian lawyer with a longstanding interest in the whole Himalayan region, offers his personal view of the situation, and concludes that the long-term solution is a reunification of India and Pakistan. He is particularly concerned about the threat that might be posed by China if the issue remains unresolved. Half the book consists of statements solicited by the author from distinguished public figures, lawyers and retired civil servants on their views of the subject. Although a very mixed bag, there are some interesting insights to be derived.

209 Contemporary South Asia. Kashmir Special Issue.

Vol. 4, no. 1 (March 1995).

This useful collection includes seven contributions on different aspects of the crisis. Edward Desmond takes a pessimistic view of the prospects for peace, based on his observation of the early stages of the insurgency from 1989 to 1991 and extensive interviews with political and government figures. Other authors contribute detailed pieces on diplomatic and political history (Gowher Rizvi, Yunus Samad), and the more general political and sociological background (Riyaz Punjabi, Balraj Puri, Mehtab Ali Shah, Reeta Chowdhari Tremblay).

210 Secular crown on fire: the Kashmir problem.
Edited by Asghar Ali Engineer. Delhi: Ajanta Publications, 1991. 344p. bibliog.

A collection of articles on the crisis, published in the Indian daily and weekly press in 1990. Some of the authors are leading journalists, others commentators and politicians with a special interest in Kashmir. Most of the writers share Engineer's own view that Kashmiri Muslims want to remain part of a secular India.

211 The crisis in Kashmir: portents of war, hopes of peace.
Šumit Ganguly. Cambridge, England: Cambridge University Press, 1997. 182p. maps.

Ganguly, a major authority on the Indo-Pakistan conflict, presents his considered views on the Kashmir conflict and its possible solutions. Compared to his earlier work (*The origins of war in South Asia: Indo-Pakistani conflicts since 1947* [Boulder, Colorado: Westview Press, 1994. 2nd ed.]), he gives greater weight here to the ethnic dimension of the conflict, that is to the internal developments within Kashmir over the fifty years since 1947, but nevertheless sees Pakistani involvement as the precipitating factor in the uprising itself. The work is valuable for Ganguly's detailed discussion of Kashmir's internal politics during the 1970s and 1980s, and for the way he considers Delhi's handling of the situation in Kashmir during that period to have been flawed. Even so, he considers that there are some possibilities of an 'internal' solution to the crisis.

212 Kashmir: the wailing vale.
Institute of Kashmir Studies. Srinagar, India: Institute of Kashmir Studies, 1995. 134p.

This book professes to be a report on human rights violations committed by the Indian forces during April-May 1995, and consists of details of numerous individual cases of killings and arbitrary arrests where such violations are claimed to have happened. The report also covers the destruction of the shrine at Charar-i-Sharief, here blamed on the Indian army.

213 1996 Lok Sabha elections in Kashmir (under the shadow of gun): the Gordian knot cut at last.
Institute of Kashmir Studies. Srinagar, India: Institute of Kashmir Studies, 1996. 114p.

This is a highly critical and polemical account of the 1996 elections, which sets out to show how coercion was used to secure a high turnout. The pamphlet also focuses on the role of 'renegade' militants, recruited by the Indian state to work against their former comrades.

214 The lost rebellion: Kashmir in the nineties.
Manoj Joshi. Delhi: Penguin Books, 1999. 483p. maps.

Written by a leading Indian journalist and defence expert, this book aims to be a history of the insurgency from 1989 up to the 1996 elections and the return to power of Farooq Abdullah. On the one hand Joshi pins responsibility for much of the violence on Pakistani involvement, on the other he is sharply critical of many aspects of India's handling of Kashmiri affairs.

215 Journal of Peace Studies.
Delhi: Centre for Peace Studies, 1993- .
Published six times a year and edited by a prominent Kashmiri academic, Riyaz Punjabi, this is an academic journal intended for a broader audience. The primary focus is on Kashmir, and beyond that on Indo-Pakistan relations, but there are frequent comparative and theoretical articles as well. The editorial 'line' favours a solution based on greater autonomy for Kashmir (and other states) within India. There are occasional articles on contemporary Kashmiri literature.

216 Kashmir: the troubled frontiers.
Afsir Karim.   Delhi: Lancer Publishers; London and Hartford, Wisconsin: Spantech & Lancer, 1994. 396p. maps. bibliog.
Written by a retired Indian army general and a group of colleagues (headed by Bharat Verma, also a former officer, and Manvendra Singh, a journalist), this adopts a critical approach to past Indian policy over the issue. It argues, for example, that India should not have given such importance to the political role of Sheikh Abdullah and Farooq Abdullah, and that political considerations more generally have been allowed to outweigh the requirements of military security and national interest. Other works have taken a similar approach, but this is notable for the coolness of its analysis and the nuancing of its concrete proposals for India's future policy designed to ensure the defeat of militancy and the region's full integration into India.

217 Beyond terrorism: new hope for Kashmir.
Salman Khurshid.   Delhi: UBSPD, 1994. 161p.
The author was a government minister in the early 1990s and one of the most senior Muslims within the Congress Party. This book covers recent Kashmiri history, the Hazratbal siege in 1993 (in which a group of Islamic militants seized control of a mosque in Srinagar), and the confrontation at a UN meeting in Geneva the following year over the human rights situation in Kashmir, in which Khurshid was one of the Indian team that scored a diplomatic victory over Pakistan. His position is that even if occasional abuses on the part of the Indian security forces occur, they are dealt with properly by internal mechanisms, and that the real abuses are committed by the various militant groups.

218 Kashmir: Pakistan's proxy war.
D. P. Kumar.   Delhi: Har-Anand Publications, c. 1994. 320p.
The author, a veteran journalist, provides a robust account of what he regards as Pakistan's continuous effort to seize Kashmir from India. Having failed to achieve its objectives in 1947-48 and in 1965, Pakistan then resorted to sponsoring low-intensity guerrilla conflict as a means to wear India out. The author takes for granted the accuracy of reports concerning 'Operation Topac', allegedly the Pakistani blueprint for launching such a conflict. He gives substantial detail, presumably derived from official Indian sources, on the location of training camps in Pakistan and the role in particular of the Inter-Services Intelligence (ISI) organization.

219 Crescent over Kashmir: politics of mullaism.
Anil Maheshwari.   Delhi: Rupa, 1993. 303p. map.
The author served in Kashmir as a journalist working for the *Hindustan Times*, a leading English-language daily newspaper published from Delhi. After a little historical

background, the main focus of the book is the exodus of the Pandit community in 1990, which he attributes to the activities of the militant groups. Extensive appendices document the violence described in the text. He criticizes the naivety of human rights activists and some of his fellow-journalists.

220 Kashmir dispute: a stalemate or solution?
Iftikhar H. Malik. *Journal of South Asian and Middle Eastern Studies*, vol. 16, no. 4 (1993), p. 55-72.

A general review of the situation in Kashmir by a prominent Pakistani scholar, which sees it as a case of ethno-nationalism. The author ends with a review of possible solutions and calls on India to show imagination and boldness in a search for peace.

221 Double betrayal: repression and insurgency in Kashmir.
Paula R. Newberg. Washington, DC: Carnegie Endowment for International Peace, 1995. 74p. map.

Based on visits to Kashmir in the early 1990s, this is a study of the conflict that seeks to bring out both the political background and the human costs involved. The author believes that even though the Indian government may defeat the militants, it cannot crush the underlying desire in the state for self-determination.

222 Kashmir: towards insurgency.
Balraj Puri. Hyderabad, India: Orient Longman; London: Sangam Books, 1993. 107p. bibliog. (Tracts for the Times, no. 4).

Balraj Puri is both a leading commentator on the affairs of Jammu and Kashmir and a political activist who has been arguing for many years the need for a non-sectarian solution to the state's problems, based on Kashmiriyat (a sense of regional identity grounded in non-religious symbols like language or in syncretic religious traditions) and on a high degree of autonomy for the state within the Indian Union. This pamphlet summarizes Kashmir's history since 1947 before discussing the insurgency and its impact on human rights in the state. A final chapter sets out Puri's own perspective.

223 Kashmir – distortions and reality.
Dina Nath Raina. Delhi: Reliance Publishing House, 1994. 307p.

This is essentially a view of the Kashmir crisis through the eyes of a member of the Pandit community and in language which borrows from Hindu nationalist perspectives. He sees Kashmir as the epitome of Indian heritage, but as constantly threatened by exclusivist Muslim attitudes both in the past and present. He argues that Muslim politicians come largely from the valley and represent only their own concerns. He lists militant attacks on members of the Pandit community in the early stages of the uprising, and is critical of international human rights organizations.

224 Report.
Jammu, India: Panun Kashmir Movement, 1995. 309p.

The text of a report on human rights violations in Kashmir submitted by the leading organization of the Pandit community to India's National Human Rights Commission in December 1995. It details the destruction of temples, the forced expulsion of the Pandits, and the poor conditions experienced in the refugee camps. An earlier, much shorter pamphlet along similar lines was produced by the Jammu Kashmir Sahayata Samiti: *Genocide of Hindus in Kashmir* (Delhi: Suruchi Prakashan, 1991).

225 Kashmir: a tragedy of errors.
Tavleen Singh. Delhi: Viking, 1995. 254p. map. bibliog.

A lively analysis of the background to the 1989 crisis and the subsequent conflict by a prominent Indian journalist. After a general introduction to Kashmir, she traces the political history of the period after Farooq Abdullah, whom she knows well, came to power in 1982. Her thesis, shared by many other writers, is that Kashmiris were progressively alienated by petty and short-sighted actions taken by Delhi politicians who were unwilling to allow the state any real autonomy, and after 1989 by heavy-handed security tactics. She also writes of the way prejudices have taken root in the popular mind about the 'untrustworthiness' of the Kashmiri Muslims.

226 Perspectives on Kashmir: the roots of conflict in South Asia.
Edited by Raju Thomas. Boulder, Colorado; San Francisco; Oxford: Westview Press, 1992. 422p.

This is a collection of essays put together in the early 1990s, just after the outbreak of the insurgency, to illustrate as wide a range of South Asian positions as possible. The quality of the contributions varies, but there are some important pieces, for example Ashutosh Varshney's article on the clash of perceptions of nationalism between the Indian, Pakistani and Kashmiri perspectives and Leo E. Rose on the politics of Azad Kashmir. An article by Kaul and Teng focuses on the suffering of the Pandit community.

227 Nation, identity and the intervening role of the state: a study of the secessionist movement in Kashmir.
Reeta Chowdhari Tremblay. *Pacific Affairs*, vol. 69, no. 4 (1997), p. 471-97.

The author links the origins of the crisis in Kashmir to the political management strategies of the Indian state. By concentrating on repression and political patronage as a twin-track approach, peace and stability can be ensured in the short term, but at a cost of the type of upsurge of popular discontent that occurred in 1989.

228 Important events in Kashmir.
Vijaya R. Trivedi. Delhi: Mohit Publications, 1994. 2 vols.

This is purely a compilation of items derived from the Indian press, arranged on a daily basis, and with little attempt to highlight what is of more than restricted significance. No indication of sources is given, although there is a limited index. Volume one covers the period from June 1990 to the end of October 1993; volume two goes up to December 1994.

229 India, Pakistan and Kashmir: antinomies of nationalism.
Ashutosh Varshney. *Asian Survey*, vol. 31, no. 11 (November 1991), p. 997-1,019.

Varshney identifies three conflicting nationalisms: secular nationalism from the Indian side, religious nationalism from the Pakistani side, and ethnic nationalism in Kashmir itself. Each has its own distinctive view of the future that is incompatible with the others.

Following a review of the issue since 1947, the author concludes that any solution would require active participation and willingness to compromise by the leaders of all three sides.

230 Kashmir: from autonomy to azadi.
Compiled by Gull Mohd. Wani.   Srinagar, India: Valley Book House, 1996. 446p.

This is a compilation of press clippings from the Indian and (to a lesser extent) the Pakistani press in the early 1990s, designed to illustrate the range of opinion that exists on the Kashmir question rather than to put forward any one position. The extracts are arranged thematically and are preceded by a general introduction and followed by appendices that give additional background material, for example on anti-terrorist legislation applicable to Jammu and Kashmir.

Kashmir and International Relations

231 Pakistan and the West: the first decade 1947-1957.
Farooq Naseem Bajwa.   Karachi, Pakistan: Oxford University
Press, 1996. 268p. maps. bibliog.
Bajwa's careful historical study looks in detail at Pakistan's decision to enter the American-led alliance systems of the Cold War, CENTO (Central Treaty Organization, originally the Baghdad Pact) and SEATO (South-East Asia Treaty Organization). He shows how these decisions were largely driven by concerns over India and Kashmir, even though when it came to the point, the alliance with the West was of little practical use in these respects. Key documents are included as appendices.

232 Pakistan's foreign policy: an historical analysis.
S. M. Burke.   London: Oxford University Press, 1973. 432p.
bibliog.
A standard history of Pakistan's foreign policy by a former Pakistani diplomat. Burke organizes his material into three periods: 1947-53, the non-aligned years; 1954-62, the aligned years; and 1963-70, a period of reappraisal. A brief postscript covers the period up to July 1972 and the Simla agreement. The focus of the book is very much on Indo-Pakistan relations, and therefore on the Kashmir question. Another book by Burke which is of interest is *Mainsprings of Indian and Pakistani foreign policies* (Minneapolis, Minnesota: University of Minnesota Press, 1974).

233 South Asian insecurity and the great powers.
Edited by Barry Buzan, Gowher Rizvi.   London: Macmillan, 1986.
257p.
The theoretical framework for this work is Buzan's concept of a security complex as an appropriate unit of analysis in the field of international relations. South Asia is one such security complex and the book looks at various factors that impinge on it. These include domestic problems in India and Pakistan, and regional rivalries within South Asia, especially the Indo-Pakistan tension with its focus on Kashmir. The editors conclude,

however, that even a solution to Kashmir would not eliminate the structural rivalry between the two countries.

234 Islamic nations and Kashmir problem.
Attar Chand.   Delhi: Raj Publications, 1994. 301p.

This book is addressed to policymakers in both India and the US, and reviews the Kashmir situation in the light of developments in the Middle East in the wake of the 1991 Gulf War and the Israeli-PLO agreement. The discussion leads the author to suggest a pro-Indian stance by the US on the Kashmir question, although the argument of the book is not always entirely clear. Appendices give the text of some sixty-nine relevant documents and news items.

235 Perspectives on Pakistan's foreign policy.
Edited by Surendra Chopra.   Amritsar, India: Guru Nanak Dev University Press, 1983. 476p.

The twenty-six articles included in this work, all but two by Indian scholars, arose out of a seminar in 1982. Some are general in scope, others provide detailed case studies. Kashmir features in many of the contributions, especially those dealing with Pakistan's relations with other countries such as Iran and other Muslim states.

236 Pakistan's relations with India: 1947-1966.
G. W. Choudhury.   London: Pall Mall Press, 1968. 341p. bibliog.

A careful and meticulous history of the subject by a political scientist who was also a minister in the government of Yahya Khan. Although written from a Pakistani perspective, it seeks to provide an essentially factual account. Kashmir is naturally central to the work. The book ends with the 1965 war. Choudhury's later book, *India, Pakistan, Bangladesh, and the major powers: politics of a divided subcontinent* (New York: The Free Press; London: Collier Macmillan, 1975) also deals at length with the Kashmir issue.

237 The security of South Asia: American and Asian perspectives.
Edited by Stephen Philip Cohen.   Urbana, Illinois; Chicago: University of Illinois Press, 1987. 290p.

The editor, himself a major figure in the field, brought together leading academic and professional experts in the diplomatic field to look at the issues in South Asian security, especially relating to Indo-Pakistan relations and to South Asia and the United States. The emphasis was on trying to take as broad a perspective as possible. The Kashmir dispute features in a number of places.

238 Himalayan battleground: Sino-Indian rivalry in Ladakh.
Margaret W. Fisher, Leo E. Rose, Robert A. Huttenback.   London: Pall Mall Press, 1963. 205p. maps.

This is the standard account of the place of Ladakh in the history of the Himalayan region. The three authors, based at the University of California, Berkeley, trace the area's history back to around 600 CE, although the larger part of the book concentrates on the period after the middle of the 19th century and after Indian independence, when China claimed the territory on the basis of its cultural affinity to Tibet. It is no coincidence that the book was written at the time of the 1962 Sino-Indian war.

239 Kashmir: a study in India-Pakistan relations.
Sisir Gupta. London: Asia Publishing House, 1966. 511p. bibliog.
This is the most authoritative statement from an Indian writer on Kashmir and a work whose careful analysis of all aspects of the situation makes it invaluable for any serious student of the subject. Gupta traces the course of the conflict from the period just before independence, through the tangled events of the 1947-49 period and the initial involvement of the United Nations, to the stalemate in the 1950s. A final chapter reviews possible ways forward. The work was completed before the 1965 war, but Gupta reviews its implications in a brief preface.

240 Pakistan in a changing world: essays in honour of K. Sarwar Hasan.
Edited by Masuma Hasan. Karachi, Pakistan: Pakistan Institute of International Affairs, 1978. 258p. maps.
Seven Pakistani and four foreign scholars contributed to this volume in honour of the founder-secretary of the Pakistan Institute of International Affairs. Kashmir is the focus of Wayne Wilcox's piece on the 1965 war, and the state features in many of the other contributions.

241 The state of martial rule: the origins of Pakistan's political economy of defence.
Ayesha Jalal. Cambridge, England: Cambridge University Press, 1990. 360p. bibliog.
The argument of this innovative work is that the structure of the Pakistan state, with its strong military element, was forged in the years immediately after independence. The conflict with India over Kashmir, and the need for allies, played a significant role in that process.

242 Soviet-Pakistan relations and post-Soviet dynamics, 1947-92.
Hafeez Malik. London: Macmillan Press, 1994. 383p.
While Pakistan's relations with the United States have always been the key to its diplomatic strategy to bring pressure on India, the country's leaders also had to take account of the Soviet Union, which in general supported the Indian stance. At certain key moments, especially after the 1965 war, the Soviet government played a significant role in events. Malik's authoritative account reviews the relationship.

243 The Indus rivers: a study of the effects of partition.
Aloys Arthur Michel. New Haven, Connecticut; London: Yale University Press, 1967. 595p. maps. bibliog.
The Indus Waters Treaty of 1960, concluded with the help of the World Bank, brought to an end years of uncertainty and recrimination between India and Pakistan over the use for irrigation of the Indus and its tributaries, most of which originate or pass through Jammu and Kashmir but pay no heed to the boundaries established in 1947. Michel's study traces the development of irrigation in the region before 1947, the political consequences of partition in 1947, the framing of the treaty and its subsequent implementation in the two countries. He notes that the treaty has survived the conflicts over Kashmir, primarily because it is clearly in the interests of both sides to leave the settlement undisturbed. A

detailed account of the negotiations that produced the treaty is *Indus waters treaty: an exercise in international mediation*, by Niranjan D. Gulhati (Bombay, India: Allied Publishers, 1973). Gulhati was head of the Indian negotiators during the critical stages. Both his and Michel's works include the text of the treaty.

244   Pakistan Horizon.
Karachi: Pakistan Institute of International Affairs, 1948- . quarterly.

This is the main journal in Pakistan devoted to Pakistan's international relations. As well as research articles on a range of specific and more general topics, each issue includes a chronology, 'Pakistan and the world', and copies of selected documents relevant to Pakistan. Pakistan's relations with India, and thus in many cases the Kashmir question, feature frequently, as for example in a special Kashmir issue in 1990 (vol. 43, no. 2). The parallel Indian journal is *India Quarterly*, published by the Indian Council on World Affairs. Both journals are non-official but represent broadly an 'establishment' view of each country's position.

245   Anglo-Pakistan relations, 1947-1976.
M. Aslam Qureshi.   Lahore, Pakistan: Research Society of Pakistan, 1976. 395p. bibliog. (Publications of the Research Society, no. 38 [sic, in fact 33]).

Originally a doctoral thesis, this work describes in detail relations between the two countries as they emerged from the trauma of partition in 1947. Kashmir inevitably looms large in the story. Another published thesis which covers some of the same ground and has a lengthy chapter on Kashmir is *Partition and Anglo-Pakistan relations, 1947-51* by Massarrat Sohail (Lahore, Pakistan: Vanguard, 1991).

246   The frontiers of Pakistan: a study of frontier problems in Pakistan's foreign policy.
Mujtaba Razvi.   Karachi, Pakistan; Dhaka: National Publishing House, 1971. 339p. maps. bibliog.

A comprehensive analysis from a Pakistani perspective of the country's frontiers, based largely on historical and geographical material. The author sees Pakistan as especially concerned to finalize its 'territorial personality', the limits of which had been somewhat hazy at the time of independence owing to the British imperial policy of relying on buffer zones. Kashmir is of central importance in this process and a substantial portion of the book is devoted to its history, especially in terms of Pakistan's diplomatic history.

247   Pakistan and the geostrategic environment: a study of foreign policy.
Hasan-Askari Rizvi.   London: Macmillan, 1993. 195p.

Rizvi's work has many references to Kashmir as a factor in Pakistan's foreign policy, both with specific reference to India, and also in the context of its relations with other countries such as China. Rizvi's earlier work on the Pakistan army is also relevant: *The military and politics in Pakistan, 1947-86* (Lahore, Pakistan: Progressive Publishers, 1986. 3rd ed.).

248 The foreign policy of Pakistan: ethnic impacts on diplomacy, 1971-1994.
Mehtab Ali Shah.   London, New York: I. B. Tauris, 1997. 267p. map. bibliog.

This book is devoted to the proposition that Pakistan's foreign policy has been driven by the interests and outlook of its majority community, namely the Punjabis, and that this has led to the absolute priority accorded to the Kashmir question. Shah considers that the other regions of the country take a different and more nuanced view, seeing a Kashmiri demand for autonomy from both India and Pakistan as in line, for example, with the Sindhi demand for autonomy.

249 Central Asia and Kashmir: a study in the context of Anglo-Russian rivalry.
K. N. Warikoo.   Delhi: Gian Publishing House, 1989. 264p. map. bibliog.

In this detailed study, the author sees the Kashmir region as the major link throughout history between South and Central Asia. During the 19th century its importance was heightened because of Anglo-Russian rivalry in the whole area. Based on an intensive study of Indian records, Warikoo's work covers the period from the end of the 18th century until the 1917 Russian revolution and its immediate aftermath. He shows how traditional links were disrupted by rivalry between the two imperial powers.

250 India-Pakistan relations 1962-1969.
Denis Wright.   Delhi: Sterling Publishing House, 1989. 152p. bibliog.

A detailed historical account which demonstrates the extent to which each country was obsessed by the other, and therefore the way in which the Kashmir dispute focused their concerns. Wright also investigates the way that the policies of the major powers conditioned the conflict, although they left its basic structure untouched.

Biographies and Autobiographies

251 Flames of the Chinar: an autobiography.
Sheikh Mohammad Abdullah, translated from Urdu by Khushwant Singh.   Delhi: Penguin Books, 1993. 176p.

This is a substantially abridged version of the Urdu original, which was dictated by Sheikh Abdullah at the end of his life. Except for a few pages at the end, the narrative ends with his second arrest and imprisonment in 1965. The autobiography, which has been fluently translated by the well-known writer Khushwant Singh, is a major source for any study of 20th-century Kashmiri history. *The Testament of Sheikh Abdullah* (Dehra Dun, Delhi: Palit & Palit, 1974) reproduces an extended interview given by Sheikh Abdullah on his release from prison in 1968, and is another important document, while he also wrote a frequently quoted statement of his position at about that time: 'Kashmir, India and Pakistan', *Foreign Affairs*, vol. 43, no. 3 (April 1965).

252 Ahead of his times: Prem Nath Bazaz: his life and times.
Nagin Bazaz.   Delhi: Sterling Publishers, 1983. 221p. bibliog.

Bazaz was born in 1905 and, as a member of the Pandit community with socialist and secularist leanings, found himself torn in different directions during his long life. An ally of Sheikh Abdullah at one point, Bazaz also found himself at odds with him at other times. This biography by his son discusses his life as a politician, author and journalist.

253 Life and times of Maharaja Ranbir Singh (1830-1885).
Sukhdev Singh Charak.   Jammu, India: Jay Kay Book House, 1985. 388p. bibliog.

Based on Persian and English sources, this is a biography of Ranbir Singh, son of Gulab Singh. He succeeded to the throne on his father's abdication in 1856 and Charak portrays him as the man who consolidated the state after the initial phase of expansion.

254 Outside the archives.
Y. D. Gundevia. Hyderabad, India: Orient Longman, 1984. 437p.
The author was a senior civil servant and diplomat who eventually became head of India's foreign service. He was close to Nehru, and was closely involved in the discussions with Pakistan in 1962-63 prompted by Britain and the US in the aftermath of the war with China, and again in 1964, when Sheikh Abdullah was allowed to go to meet President Ayub Khan. In his memoirs he devotes considerable space to these meetings and to expounding his personal view that India should have taken a pragmatic approach based on recognition of a partitioned Kashmir with some limited territorial concessions to Pakistan. Gundevia also contributed an extended postscript or memoir to *The Testament of Sheikh Abdullah* (Dehra Dun, Delhi: Palit & Palit, 1974).

255 Shabir Shah: a living legend in Kashmir history.
Altaf Hussain. Srinagar, India: Noble Publishing House, 1995. 2nd ed. 187p.
This is an admiring biography of Shabir Shah, a prominent activist and founder of the Jammu and Kashmir People's League who was imprisoned on many occasions by the Indian authorities. His demand is self-determination for the whole of Jammu and Kashmir.

256 My frozen turbulence in Kashmir.
Jagmohan. Delhi: Allied Publishers, 1991. 723p. map.
Jagmohan was a highly controversial civil servant who served two terms as Governor of Jammu and Kashmir, first from 1984 to 1989, and then for a few months in 1990 before he was removed. His critics see him as anti-Muslim and anti-Kashmiri. He is identified with a strong centralist approach, and in his book sees the whole Indian polity, not just Kashmir, as in need of radical overhaul. He was responsible for the disputed dismissal of Farooq Abdullah in 1984. The book offers a detailed description and justification of his actions throughout his term in office.

257 The tūzuk-i-Jahāngīrī or memoirs of Jahāngīr.
Jahangir, translated by Alexander Rogers, edited by Henry Beveridge. Delhi: Munshiram Manoharlal, 1968. 2 vols.
The emperor Jahangir, son of Akbar, consolidated his father's achievements in India. He was particularly fond of Kashmir, visited it as often as possible, and was responsible for several of its monuments. The memoirs, originally written in Persian and first published in the present translation in 1909-14, are readable and personal in tone. The second volume contains an extended account of his visit in 1620. The standard account of Jahangir's reign is by Beni Prasad (*History of Jahangir* [London: Oxford University Press, 1922]).

258 Autumn leaves: Kashmiri reminiscences.
Ram Nath Kak. Delhi: Vitasta, 1995. 126p.
A charming and guileless memoir by a Kashmiri Pandit from his childhood in the 1920s and 1930s to his successful career as a veterinary surgeon, during which he was posted in various places throughout the state.

259 Maharaja Hari Singh (1895-1961).
Edited by M. L. Kapur.   Delhi: Har-Anand Publications, 1995.
233p.

This is a compilation of centenary tributes to the life and work of the last Maharaja of Kashmir. Contributors, mainly academics and public figures, emphasize his work in the fields of social reform. There are also more personal tributes, including one from his golf professional. The chapter by Ghansar Singh is a first-hand account of events in Gilgit in 1947.

260 Looking back: the autobiography of Mehr Chand Mahajan, former chief justice of India.
Mehr Chand Mahajan.   London: Asia Publishing House, 1963.
299p.

Born in the Punjab, Mehr Chand Mahajan was a distinguished lawyer who eventually became Chief Justice of India. He became a judge before independence and was a member in 1947 of the Boundary Commission under Sir Cyril Radcliffe. He was then, at the instance it is usually thought of Vallabhbhai Patel, appointed Prime Minister of the state of Jammu and Kashmir in September 1947, and during the last hectic days before 26 October, attempted unsuccessfully to mediate an agreed accession of the state to India. His memoirs are critical of Sheikh Abdullah, who succeeded him as Prime Minister and whom he regarded as 'thirsty for power'. The book contains some useful information on the progress of events at the time of accession, and has often been quoted by scholars.

261 Sir George Cunningham: a memoir.
Norval Mitchell.   Edinburgh, London: William Blackwood, 1968.
183p. map.

Governor of the North-West Frontier Province at the time of independence, Cunningham remained in post until April 1948 during the early stages of the Kashmir crisis, in which he played a significant role. With the help of Cunningham's diary, Mitchell gives a detailed account of the way Cunningham responded to the complex pressures to which he was subject as a servant of the new state of Pakistan.

262 The founding of the Kashmir state: a biography of Maharajah Gulab Singh, 1792-1858.
K. M. Panikkar.   London: George Allen & Unwin, 1953. 172p.
map.

First published in 1930 as *Gulab Singh*, this is an admiring but scholarly biography of the founder of the state of Jammu and Kashmir. Gulab Singh (who in fact died in 1857 not 1858) was the Dogra ruler of Jammu who succeeded by skilful manoeuvring between the British East India Company on the one hand and the Sikh kingdom of Lahore in its last days on the other to buy Kashmir from the former. Panikkar spent much of his life as a senior official in various princely states, and was anxious to ensure that their side of the picture was presented. Gulab Singh has generally been given a bad press by the British, with whom he dealt over the treaty of Amritsar, and by other writers who have seen him as cruel, amoral and greedy. Panikkar by contrast sees him as a wise and farseeing statesman. A more recent biography of Gulab Singh is by Bawa Satinder Singh (*The Jammu fox: a biography of Maharaja Gulab Singh of Kashmir, 1792-1857* [Carbondale,

Illinois: Southern Illinois University Press; London: Feffer & Simons, 1974]). Singh's work, originally a doctoral thesis, aims at a more rounded account of his subject, although his final assessment is distinctly negative.

263 Memoirs of Alexander Gardner.
Edited by Hugh Pearse. Edinburgh, London: William Blackwood & Sons, 1898. 359p.

Alexander Gardner was a colonel in the Kashmir army and, by his own account at least, the most remarkable of all the European soldiers of fortune who served in the army of Ranjit Singh during the first half of the nineteenth century. While the bulk of his memoirs cover his time in the Punjab, the last section covers the part of his life after 1851 when he served Gulab Singh in Kashmir. However, a later work, *European adventurers of northern India, 1785 to 1849*, C. Grey, edited by H. L. O. Garrett (Lahore: Superintendent, Government Printing, 1929) persuasively portrays him as a Baron Münchausen figure who borrowed most of his material from other people. His time in Kashmir is better documented than the rest and has some interest.

264 My life and times.
Mir Qasim. Delhi: Allied Publishers, 1992. 319p.

Mir Qasim was a major Kashmiri politician in the 1960s and 1970s, and was chief minister of the state at the point when Sheikh Abdullah made his deal with Mrs Gandhi in 1975. A former associate of Abdullah, he played a role in the negotiations that led up to the deal. Later on, he left Congress and joined the opposition. Inevitably, some of his autobiography is devoted to settling scores and blaming Congress for the outbreak of the insurgency in 1989.

265 Gulabnama of Diwan Kirpa Ram: a history of Maharaja Gulab Singh of Jammu and Kashmir.
Diwan Kirpa Ram, translated and annotated by Sukhdev Singh Charak. Delhi: Light and Life Publishers, 1977. 462p.

Gulab Singh succeeded in founding the state of Jammu and Kashmir by his skill in manoeuvring between the Sikh rulers of Punjab and the British East India Company, at this point in its period of aggressive expansion. Diwan Kirpa Ram was his chief officer and thus in a position to write from direct experience. The *Gulabnama* was written in Persian in the form of a panegyric, but nevertheless contains important source material about the formation of Jammu and Kashmir in its present form. The translator, a professional historian, has provided a useful introduction as well as extensive annotations to the text.

266 Autobiography (1931-1967).
Karan Singh. Delhi: Oxford University Press, 1989. 337p.

Karan Singh was the son of Hari Singh, the last ruler of Jammu and Kashmir, and himself the Sadar-i-Riyasat, or governor, of the state for a number of years after 1947. He is also a distinguished scholar who has played a part in national politics. His autobiography is carefully written and contains detailed accounts of his close interaction with Nehru and Sheikh Abdullah, although he avoids comments that might be seen as controversial. The early chapters are also interesting for their insights into life as a member of a leading princely family in the last years of British rule. The autobiography was originally issued in two volumes: the first, *Heir Apparent* (Delhi: Oxford University Press) in 1953, and the second, *Sadar-i-Riyasat* (ibid.) in 1985.

267 Farooq Abdullah: Kashmir's prodigal son.
Aditya Sinha.   Delhi: UBSPD, 1996. 256p. bibliog.

A journalistic account with extensive sections on the more colourful aspects of Farooq Abdullah's career. It also provides a broad coverage of his career set against the general political history of the 1980s and 1990s. Sinha is broadly sympathetic to Farooq Abdullah's desire to obtain greater autonomy for Kashmir, and sees him as likely to play a central role in the future.

268 Tyndale-Biscoe of Kashmir: an autobiography.
C. E. Tyndale-Biscoe.   London: Seeley, Service, [1951]. 280p.

Canon Tyndale-Biscoe taught as a missionary in Kashmir for over fifty years, leaving at independence. In that time he became a local institution, as Sheikh Abdullah's foreword to the book indicates. His autobiography reveals his total dedication to the school he established and the boys he taught.

Population

General

269 Ethnische Anthropologie von Afghanistan, Pakistan und Kashmir. (Ethnic anthropology of Afghanistan, Pakistan and Kashmir.)
Wolfram Bernhard. Stuttgart, Germany; New York: Gustav Fischer Verlag, 1991. 282p. maps. bibliog.

This detailed work traces the movements of and relationships between the various population groups in the north west of the subcontinent and in Afghanistan, using the anthropometrical tools of physical anthropology such as blood-group mapping and skull shape. The whole of Kashmir, Ladakh and the northern areas are included but not Jammu. An English article by Bernhard sums up his general findings: 'Ethnogenesis of South Asia with special references to India', *Anthropology*, vol. 41 (1983).

270 Census of India, 1981. Series 8, Jammu and Kashmir.
Delhi: Government of India, Controller of Publications, 1981-88. 10 vols. maps.

The census of 1981, held, of course, only in the Indian-controlled section of the state, gave the total population as 6.0 million, an increase of 29.7 per cent since 1971. The ten volumes cover the standard census categories of urban/rural distribution, occupational structure, literacy rates, housing and language, as well as the specifically Indian issues of the percentages of Scheduled Castes and Tribes. No census was held in 1991 because of the uprising (the same was the case in 1951), but the projected population figure was 7.7 million. In 1998, the estimate was 9.5 million. The population growth rate is therefore at the upper end of the Indian range. In 1901, the population of those areas of the undivided state now controlled by India was 2.1 million.

271 The population of India and Pakistan.
Kingsley Davis. Princeton, New Jersey: Princeton University Press, 1951. 263p. 22 maps. bibliog.

Although specific references to Jammu and Kashmir are buried away in the individual chapters, Davis's book has been the starting point for all subsequent demographic work on the Indian subcontinent. The book reviews the nature and reliability of the historical evidence for population levels and for trends in birth and death rates and discusses social structure and change from a demographic perspective.

272 A portrait of population of Jammu and Kashmir.
V. K. Moza. Srinagar, India: Directorate of Census Operations Jammu and Kashmir, 1990. 130p. map.

A useful compendium of information drawn from the 1981 Census. The chapters cover standard census topics such as male-female and urban-rural ratios, as well as language and religion, occupational patterns and demographic trends. An earlier publication with the same title covering the 1971 census was prepared by J. N. Zutshi and published in 1974, also by the Directorate of Census Operations Jammu and Kashmir.

273 National family health survey (MCH and family planning), Jammu region of Jammu and Kashmir 1993.
Bombay, India: International Institute for Population Sciences; Srinagar, India: University of Srinagar, Population Research Centre, 1995. 282p.

The main survey covered virtually the whole of India, and was the largest such survey of its kind. However, the insurgency meant that it was impossible to hold the survey in the Kashmir portion of the state. The results for the Jammu region cover many aspects of women's health and that of their children. The results show, for example, an increase in the mean age of marriage and widespread adoption of family planning practices.

274 Census of India, 1931. Vol. 24. Jammu and Kashmir.
Anant Ram, Hira Nand Raina. Jammu, India: Government of Jammu and Kashmir, 1933. 2 parts.

Produced by the Government of Jammu and Kashmir but as part of the general census of the same year, part one of the volume gives a narrative analysis of standard demographic variables such as gender ratios, migration patterns, language and religion, while part 2 contains the tables, in many cases analysed down to district level. The first census to be held in Jammu and Kashmir was conducted in 1891.

Overseas populations

275 South Asians overseas: migration and ethnicity.
Edited by Colin Clarke, Ceri Peach, Steven Vertovec. Cambridge, England: Cambridge University Press, 1990. 375p. maps. bibliog.

The main interest here is the contribution by Roger Ballard in which he compares the experience of Sikhs from Jullundur (in Indian Punjab) and Muslims from Mirpur (in Azad Kashmir). Much of the case study material is drawn from Bradford. Ballard shows how the two communities have followed different trajectories in relation to marriage and family, with Mirpuris maintaining closer links with their villages of origin, and relates this both to the effect of British immigration policies over the years and to cultural differences between the two groups.

276 Migrants, workers and the social order.
Edited by Jeremy Eades. London, New York: Tavistock Publications, 1987. 281p. bibliog. (ASA Monographs, no. 26).

This is a collection of papers from an academic conference of British anthropologists held in 1986 around the theme of migration. Roger Ballard's 'The political economy of migration: Pakistan, Britain, and the Middle East' focuses on migrants from the Mirpur district of Kashmir and the economic and social context in which they make decisions on migration.

277 Home from home: British Pakistanis in Mirpur.
Irna Imran, Tim Smith. Bradford, England: City of Bradford Metropolitan District Council Arts Museums and Libraries, 1997. 64p. map.

This large-format book brings together the reminiscences of some of the many Mirpuris who came to Britain after the Second World War and settled in cities like Birmingham and Bradford. Most maintained close links with their natal villages, and sent money back to buy land or build houses. The second and third generations also maintain close links and often visit. These photographs and oral histories capture, often very poignantly, the mixed feelings that their ancestral land awakens in them. Some of the migrants came originally from the area flooded by the Mangla dam in the 1950s, and there are striking pictures of mosques and houses half-submerged.

278 Islam in transition: religion and identity among British Pakistani youth.
Jessica Jacobson. London, New York: Routledge, 1998. 177p. bibliog.

Originally a doctoral thesis, this is a study of young Muslims in the Waltham Forest area of London. Many of the subjects of the book in fact belong to families who came originally from the Mirpur area. The themes of the book are how an Islamic identity has remained intact for these young people, even while its content has changed in many significant ways.

279 Britannia's crescent: making a place for Muslims in British society.
Danièle Joly. Aldershot, England: Avebury, 1995. 197p. bibliog.

A collection of mainly previously published essays that focus on different aspects of community life among Muslims in Birmingham, many of whom are of Mirpuri origin. The author worked in Birmingham in the 1980s, and she writes about the ways in which the community has become settled and the problems it has faced. Her focus is on the dynamic interaction between Muslims, drawing sustenance from their faith, and the broader institutions of British society, and she pays particular attention to the associations that have been developed to serve the community. One chapter is devoted to the results of a survey conducted among Mirpuri parents about their expectations of the local schools attended by their children.

280 Islamic Britain. Religion, politics and identity among British Muslims: Bradford in the 1990s.
Philip Lewis. London, New York: I. B. Tauris, 1994. 250p. maps.

The Yorkshire city of Bradford is home to more than 50,000 of Britain's Muslim population, and more than half that number came originally from Mirpur in Pakistan-held Kashmir. Originally a PhD thesis, this is a sympathetic treatment of the community. Lewis considers its members as belonging both to Britain and the Islamic world, and he traces the debates and actions caused by this fact, especially in the fields of education and cultural change. The agitation against Salman Rushdie's *The Satanic Verses* in the early 1990s was particularly strong in Bradford, and this also forms part of Lewis's study.

281 Minority families in Britain: support and stress.
Edited by Verity Saifullah Khan. London: Macmillan, 1979. 203p. bibliog. (Studies in Ethnicity, no. 2).

The contributors to this collection, much of which originated in a conference in 1976, are concerned to challenge popular misconceptions about the relationship between minority families and the social services, particularly those which see the former as simply generating 'problems' for the latter. The editor herself writes about Mirpuri families in Bradford, who came originally from Azad Kashmir, and she has a paper on the same topic, 'The Pakistanis: Mirpuri villagers at home and in Bradford', in *Between two cultures: migrants and minorities in Britain*, edited by James L. Watson (Oxford: Basil Blackwell, 1977, p. 57-89).

282 Punjabi identity: continuity and change.
Edited by Gurharpal Singh, Ian Talbot. Delhi: Manohar, 1996.

Nasreen Ali, Pat Ellis and Zafar Khan argue in their chapter entitled 'The 1990s: a time to separate British Punjabi and British Kashmiri identity' that within the British context migrants who came originally from Mirpur are increasingly asserting a Kashmiri identity. They suggest that events in Kashmir, especially the emergence of the Jammu and Kashmir Liberation Front, have been instrumental in this process. They criticize other writers who have too easily, they say, described Mirpuri culture as a variant of that of the neighbouring Punjab. Ellis and Khan make related arguments in another article, 'Partition and Kashmir: implications for the region and the diaspora', in *Region and partition: Bengal, Punjab and the partition of the subcontinent*, edited by Ian Talbot and Gurharpal Singh (Karachi, Pakistan: Oxford University Press, 1999).

Languages and Dialects

283 Languages of Northern Areas.
Peter C. Backstrom, Carla F. Radloff.   Islamabad: National Institute
of Pakistan Studies and Summer Institute of Linguistics, 1992. 417p.
bibliog. (Sociolinguistic Survey of Northern Pakistan, Vol. 2).

This survey reports on detailed fieldwork carried out in the Northern Areas. Backstrom
reports on Balti, Burushaski, Wakhi and Domaaki, while Radloff writes on the dialects of
Shina. The emphasis of all the chapters is as much on sociolinguistic as on descriptive
questions.

**284 The pronunciation of Kashmiri: Kashmiri sounds, how to make
them and how to transcribe them.**
T. Grahame Bailey.   London: Royal Asiatic Society, 1937. 70p.
(James G. Forlong Fund, Vol. 16).

A practical guide both to the basics and to the finer points of Kashmiri pronunciation
based on the speech of three Kashmiris from Srinagar, including T. N. Kaul, later to be
India's Foreign Secretary. The book uses the International Phonetic Association's system
for transcription.

**285 Die Burushaski-Sprache von Hunza und Nager. (The Burushaski
language of Hunza and Nager).**
Hermann Berger.   Wiesbaden, Germany: Harrassowitz Verlag,
1998. 3 vols. (Neuindische Studien, 13).

This extensive study of Burushaski includes a grammar, transcribed and translated
extracts of everyday speech, and a German-Burushaski-German dictionary.

286   A dictionary of the Kashmiri language.
George A. Grierson, from materials compiled by Īśvara Kaula.
Calcutta, India: Asiatic Society of Bengal, 1916-32. 1,252p.
(Bibliotheca Indica).

This monumental work, published in several parts but with continuous pagination, has been at the root of all subsequent research on Kashmiri. As Grierson makes plain in his introduction, the dictionary originated in Ishwar Kaula's Kashmiri-Sanskrit dictionary, which was still in manuscript form at the time of the latter's death in 1893. The words are given in romanized transliteration and in the Devanagari script, or in the case of words borrowed from Persian, in Persian script, together with a Sanskrit equivalent and an English translation, with gloss where necessary.

287   Linguistic survey of India.
George Abraham Grierson.   Calcutta, India: Government of India, Central Publications Branch, 1903-19. 11 vols. (some in multiple parts). maps. bibliog.

Although out of date in many important respects, Grierson's work, carried out in the late 19th and early 20th centuries, is still the starting point for linguistic research on South Asia. The first volume (in three parts) provides a general and comparative survey of the subject and establishes the classificatory scheme. Each volume in turn then deals with the languages in each of the groups identified. For each one there are carefully recorded and analysed specimens and brief accounts of grammar, syntax and a limited vocabulary. Kashmiri, regarded by Grierson as a Dardic language, although strongly influenced by Indo-Aryan languages, is covered in the second part of volume eight. Languages and dialects spoken in other parts of the region – the Punjabi dialects spoken in Jammu, or the Burushaski language of the Hunza area, are covered in other volumes in accordance with Grierson's linguistic classification. Grierson's specialist essays on Kashmiri grammar were brought together in a single volume, *Essays on Kashmiri grammar* (London: Luzac; Calcutta: Thacker, Spink & Co., 1899), while his two-volume *A manual of the Kāshmīrī language* (Oxford: Clarendon Press, 1911) combines the functions of a systematic grammar, phrase-book and Kashmiri-English vocabulary.

288   Aspects of Kashmiri linguistics.
Edited by Omkar N. Koul, Peter Edwin Hook.   Delhi: Bahri Publications, 1984. 172p. bibliog. (Series in Indian Languages and Linguistics, no. 12).

This volume of collected papers contains nine specialized contributions by academic experts. Some deal with the relationship of Kashmiri to other languages, others with aspects of syntax and morphology.

289   Kashmiri: a sociolinguistic survey.
Omkar N. Koul, Ruth Laila Schmidt.   Patiala, India: Indian Institute of Language Studies, 1983. 72p.

Based on survey data, this monograph notes that all Kashmiri-speakers have to be effectively bilingual (with Urdu) or trilingual (with Urdu and English). Kashmiri is the language of the home, the others of the public world.

290 Sociolinguistics: South Asian perspectives.
Edited by Omkar N. Koul. Delhi: Creative Books, 1995. bibliog.

The main interest here is the editor's own paper, 'Personal names in Kashmiri'. This is a detailed and valuable analysis of the often complex structure of personal names in Kashmiri. Both Muslim and Hindu systems are discussed, and there is also a section on nicknames.

291 Spoken Kashmiri: a language course.
Omkar N. Koul. Patiala, India: Indian Institute of Language Studies, 1987. 127p.

A conventional 'teach yourself' volume, organized into twenty lessons. There is little help with the pronunciation of the language, and users are advised to find a native speaker for advice. Another self-study course is that by Braj B. Kachru, *An introduction to spoken Kashmiri* (Urbana, Illinois: Department of Linguistics, University of Illinois, 1973. 2 vols.).

292 The languages and races of Dardistan.
G. W. Leitner. Lahore, Pakistan: Government Central Book Depot, 1878. 3rd ed. various pagination.

Leitner, a scholar-administrator, was one of the first Europeans to visit the regions of Gilgit, Hunza and Chitral, first in 1866 and then again in 1872, and was also a pioneer of the scientific study of the languages of the region. Although ultimately part of the Indo-European family, these are quite distinct from those of the rest of the Indian subcontinent. The present work, first published in 1877, includes sections on the dialects spoken in Gilgit, Chilas and Astor, on legends and proverbs, and on customs. There is also a translation of a contemporary text on the wars between the state of Jammu and Kashmir and the small kingdoms of the region. Much of the material in the book also appears in an earlier work by Leitner, *Results of a tour in "Dardistan, Kashmir, Little Tibet, Ladak, Zanskar etc", vol. 1* (Lahore: Indian Public Opinion Press; London: Trubner, 1868-73). Leitner's colourful career is covered in some detail by John Keay in *The Gilgit game* (see entry no. 55).

293 The Burushaski Language.
D. L. R. Lorimer. Oslo: H. Aschehoug, 1935-38. 3 vols. (Instituttet for Sammenlignende Kulturforskning, Series B, 29).

This extensive work is the first systematic study of a language spoken only in a limited area in and around Hunza and without a written tradition. Burushaski does not appear to be structurally related to any other language group. The first volume covers the grammar, the second provides samples of the language in parallel transcription and translation. The materials included cover folk tales, proverbs and folk songs. The third volume provides vocabularies. Further work on Lorimer's materials was done by a group of Norwegian linguistics specialists, Georg Morgenstierne, Hans Vogt and Carl Hj. Borgstrøm, in 'A triplet of Burushaski studies', *Norsk Tidsskrift for Sprogvidenskap*, Bind XIII (1942).

294   Report on a linguistic mission to north-western India.
Georg Morgenstierne.   Oslo: H. Aschehoug, 1932. 76p. maps.
(Instituttet for Sammenlignende Kulturforskning, Series C, III-1).

Morgenstierne was a distinguished scholar of Indo-Iranian languages. The present work
is a brief field report on a visit that he made to the Northern Areas in order to study the
languages spoken there. He was interested in the character of the languages spoken on the
frontier between the Iranian and Indo-Aryan branches of the larger Indo-European family.

295   A dictionary of Urdu, classical Hindi, and English.
John T. Platts.   London: Oxford University Press, 1930. 1,259p.

Although in most respects Platts' dictionary dates back more than a hundred years, it is
an essential tool for any serious student of the Urdu language (the official language of
Kashmir). The Urdu word is in each case given first, followed, where the word is also
used in Hindi, by its transliteration in Devanagari (the Hindi script), and then by an
English definition. Abdul Haq's dictionaries are also in common use – *The standard
English-Urdu dictionary* (Aurangabad, India: Anjuman-e-Urdu Press, 1937. 1,513p.
[Anjuman-e-Taraqqi-e-Urdu (India) Series, no. 106]), and *The standard Urdu-English
dictionary* (Delhi: Chaman Book Depot, [1978?]. 831p.).

296   Jammu, Kashmir and Ladakh: linguistic predicament.
Edited by P. N. Pushp, K. Warikoo.   Delhi: Har-Anand
Publications, 1996. 224p. map. bibliog.

A set of papers on the sociolinguistics of the Jammu and Kashmir region. The
predicament of the title refers to the importance of promoting mother-tongue education in
Kashmiri, Dogri and other local languages, and the possibility of using Devanagari script
as well as Persian for writing Kashmiri. For the authors of many of the papers, this
emphasis is linked to promoting the region's plural culture, and there is a sometimes
explicit critique of Urdu as a language of Islamic dominance. There is also criticism of
Grierson's classification of Kashmiri as a Dardic language.

297   Kashmiri for non-Kashmiries (learning and teaching problems).
Som Nath Raina.   Patiala, India: Gopi Publications, 1990. 206p.
bibliog.

Designed to help teachers, this is a technical work on the problems encountered by non-
mother tongue speakers in India who are learning Kashmiri. The main issue addressed is
'interference' from mother tongues.

298   A new course in Urdu and spoken Hindi for learners in Britain.
Ralph Russell.   London: School of Oriental and African Studies,
External Services Division, 1986. 2nd ed. 4 vols.

First published in 1980 as *A new course in Hindustani*, this is designed specifically as a
teach yourself course for adult learners in Britain. It would be useful for anyone with
limited time available. The first part contains the basic course, the second offers an
outline of the grammar, the third presents sample readings and the fourth part is devoted
to the script. Urdu is very much the lingua franca of the Muslim section of the Kashmiri
population, as well as the official language of the state.

299 Hatim's tales: Kashmiri stories and songs.
Aurel Stein, edited by George Grierson. London: John Murray,
1923. 525p. (Indian Texts Series).

Hatim, whose photograph is included as a frontispiece, was a professional storyteller and
minstrel, who was 'discovered' by Aurel Stein in 1896 in a small mountain village.
Together with Govind Kaul (to whom Stein pays an extended and graceful tribute in the
preface), Stein took down the words of twelve stories from Hatim, while the material was
later edited by Grierson, who also translated the stories into English and added a full
glossary. The format of the work is that the twelve stories are transcribed twice, once
following Stein's literal transcription and once following Kaul's version using the
Devanagari script (here in romanized form). Stein's version is accompanied by Grierson's
literary translation, while Kaul's version is accompanied by a word for word translation.
The book is equally useful as a record of folk tales recounted by a traditional bard and as
a contribution to the study of the Kashmiri language.

300 Kashmiri: a cognitive-descriptive grammar.
Kashi Wali, Omkar N. Koul. London, New York: Routledge, 1997.
378p. bibliog.

This work is one of a series of descriptive grammars intended to incorporate the findings
and terminology of modern theoretical linguistics. The work is organized into sections on
syntax, morphology and phonology. An earlier work along the same lines was *A reference
grammar of Kashmiri* by Braj B. Kachru (Urbana, Illinois: Department of Linguistics,
University of Illinois, 1969). This includes a section that reviews previous work on the
language.

301 Languages of South Asia: a guide.
G. A. Zograph, translated by G. L. Campbell. London: Routledge
& Kegan Paul, 1982. 231p. maps. bibliog. (Languages of Asia and
Africa, Vol. 3).

This is a brief but systematic description, based initially on Grierson's *Linguistic Survey
of India* (see entry no. 287), of the languages spoken in what philologists now think of as
the 'Indian linguistic area'. Zograph provides a succinct summary of present thinking on
the relationship of Kashmiri to the Dardic group of languages, as well as a description of
its phonology and morphology. The book was originally published in Russian in 1960 as
Yazyki Indii, Pakistana, Tseilona i Nepala (Languages of India, Pakistan, Ceylon and
Nepal) (Moscow: Oriental Publishing House). The *Atlas of the languages and ethnic
communities of South Asia*, by Roland J.-L. Breton (Delhi; Thousand Oaks, California;
London: Sage Publications, 1997) is useful both for its maps, showing the distribution of
languages in the Jammu and Kashmir region, and for the detailed commentaries.

Religion

302 Conversions to Islam in the valley of Kashmir.
Aziz Ahmad. *Central Asiatic Journal*, vol. 23, no. 1 (1979), p. 3-18.

The process of conversion to Islam in South Asia has been hotly debated in the past, although a consensus has emerged that in most of the region, Sufi influence was extremely important. Sufism was important in Kashmir as well, but Ahmad, a distinguished scholar of South Asian Islam, makes the point that Islam arrived from Central Asia first through trading links and then with the Mongol invasions of the 14th century, and not from the Middle East. Mass conversions followed during the reign of Sikander at the end of the century. Ahmad sees this history as explaining why Islam in the Kashmir valley has remained close to the mainstream of Sunni Islam.

303 An intellectual history of Islam in India.
Aziz Ahmad.   Edinburgh: Edinburgh University Press, 1969. 226p. bibliog. (Islamic Surveys, no. 7).

Despite the title, this work by one of the most distinguished students of the subject is really a survey of Indian Islam and the religious and spiritual tendencies within it. The major sub-groups and the Sufi orders are each described in a few pages. There are also chapters on literature and the fine arts. As well as offering a general introduction to the context of Islam in Kashmir, it also contains a number of specific references to the area.

304 Shaiva devotional songs of Kashmir: a translation and study of Utpaladeva's Shivastotravali.
Constantina Rhodes Bailly.   Albany, New York: State University of New York Press, 1987. 196p. bibliog. (SUNY Series in Kashmir Shaivism).

Utpaladeva, who flourished in the first half of the 10th century, was both a philosopher and a writer of devotional songs expressing the core ideas of Shaivism. The present work contains translations of twenty songs, the transliterated Sanskrit text and an introduction that discusses the religious ideas and the spiritual quest revealed by the poetry. There is a 1990 Indian reprint (Delhi: Sri Satguru Publications).

305 Irene Petrie: missionary to Kashmir.
Mrs Ashley Carus-Wilson (Mary Carus-Wilson). London: Hodder & Stoughton, 1900. 343p.

A classic example of the tradition of missionary biographies, designed to instruct as well as inform. The subject was a teacher who went to Kashmir under the auspices of the Church Missionary Society and taught in Srinagar before dying at Leh on a visit to the Moravian mission there, after only three years in Kashmir. She worked alongside Arthur Neve and Cecil Tyndale-Biscoe.

306 Kashmir Shaivism.
J. C. Chatterjee. Albany, New York: State University of New York Press, 1986. 175p. bibliog.

First published in 1914, the present edition has a preface by William Barnard and a foreword by Swami Muktananda, both expounding the coherence and practical relevance of Kashmir Shaivism. Chatterjee's own work was a pioneering study in the field, and describes in detail, with copious Sanskrit quotations, Shaivite doctrine concerning God's manifestation in the universe. He discusses the various *tattvas*, or principles, on which the sensible universe is constructed.

307 Rupa Bhawani (life, teachings and philosophy).
Triloki Nath Dhar. Srinagar, India: All India Saraswat Cultural Organization, Jammu and Kashmir Region, 1977. 167p.

A hagiographical work devoted to the life and poetry of the 18th-century mystic, Rupa Bhawani. The author reproduces and translates her poetry, and provides a running commentary on its spiritual meaning and significance.

308 The encyclopaedia of Islam.
Leiden, The Netherlands: E. J. Brill; London: Luzac (vols. 1-3 only), 1960- . 2nd ed.

This multi-volumed work is a major example of worldwide scholarly cooperation. Some hundreds of scholars, Muslim and non-Muslim (although the latter predominate), have contributed articles over the years to a work which covers all major events, personalities, places and themes in Islamic religion and history. There is also some coverage of economic and social issues. There is an entry on Kashmir, which summarizes the region's history, and several other relevant entries. The first edition, in five volumes, was published by E. J. Brill between 1913 and 1942. The second edition had reached six volumes by 1991 but the final work is likely to be double that number. A parallel French edition is published by E. J. Brill in partnership with G. P. Maisonneuve (Paris). There is a linked atlas, *An historical atlas of Islam*, edited by William Brice (Leiden: E. J. Brill, 1981). Another standard encyclopaedia that includes some material on Kashmir is the *Oxford encyclopaedia of the modern Islamic world*, edited by John L. Esposito (New York; Oxford: Oxford University Press, 1995. 4 vols.), although the main entry on Kashmir presents a somewhat 'Pakistani' view of the issues.

309 Body and cosmology in Kashmir Śaivism.

Gavin D. Flood. San Francisco: Mellen Research University Press, 1993. 441p. bibliog.

Originally a PhD thesis, this is a technical study of the subject. The author explores Kashmiri Shaivism through the way its texts see the human body as a consequence of, and homologous with, the cosmic bodies of Shaiva cosmology.

310 The Himalayan mission: Moravian Church centenary, Leh, Ladakh, India, 1885-1985.

Leh, India: Moravian Church, 1986. 80p.

A brochure, partly written by John Bray, to mark the centenary of the Moravian mission in Ladakh. Moravian missionaries posted in Ladakh, notably A. H. Francke, did pioneering work in the study of Tibetan language and culture. There are also sections discussing the evangelizing work of the mission.

311 The Shi'a of India.

John Norman Hollister. London: Luzac, 1953. 440p. bibliog.

Despite its age, this work by a scholar-missionary is still consulted on the subject. There is a section on Kashmir, which at times offers some rather speculative comments on the historical origins of the Shia minority among Kashmir's Muslim population.

312 Die Religionen des Hindukusch. (The religions of the Hindu Kush.)

K. Jettmar, with contributions by Schuyler Jones, Max Klimburg. Stuttgart, Germany: Verlag W. Kohlhammer, 1975. 525p. maps. bibliog. (Die Religionen der Menschheit, vol. 4, no. 1).

This is a massive, anthropologically oriented account of the religious beliefs of the non-Muslim tribal groups in the Hindu Kush mountains and neighbouring areas. For each major group of peoples, there is a description of gods, rites and festivals.

313 History of Buddhism in Kashmir.

Sarla Khosla. Delhi: Sagar Publications, 1972. 188p. bibliog.

Buddhism was present in the Kashmir region from at least the 3rd century BCE and possibly earlier, and flourished until it was gradually displaced by a reinvigorated Brahmanism towards the end of the first millennium CE. Sarla Khosla offers a general, in some places rather cursory survey of all aspects of the Buddhist tradition in the region, covering its advent and expansion, relations with other religious traditions, sculpture and literature. Another study, which deals primarily with the relationship between Buddhism and the successive rulers of the region, is *Buddhism in Kashmir* by Nalinaksha Dutt (Delhi: Eastern Book Linkers, 1985).

314 The Ahmadiyah movement: a history and perspective.

Spencer Lavan. Delhi: Manohar Book Service, 1974. 220p. bibliog.

The Ahmadiyah movement, whose adherents are also sometimes known as Qadianis, was founded by Mirza Ghulam Ahmed and is a religious reform movement within Islam that had its origins in late 19th-century Punjab. One of the tenets of Ahmadi belief is that Jesus did not die on the cross but travelled to Kashmir, where he died and was buried in Srinagar. Ahmadis were active in the 1931 agitation against the Maharaja, which in many ways marked the start of organized politics in the state. The teachings of the Ahmadiyah movement are most conveniently found in English in *Invitation to Ahmadiyyat*, by Bashir-ud-din Mahmud Ahmad (London; Boston, Massachusetts; Henley, England: Routledge & Kegan Paul, 1980 [originally published in Pakistan in 1961]).

315 Triadic mysticism: the mystical theology of the Śaivism of Kashmir.

Paul E. Murphy.   Delhi: Motilal Banarsidass, 1986. 226p. bibliog.

This is a general exposition of the philosophical system of Kashmir Shaivism and of the ways to liberation. The triad of the title refers to the three schools of theology within the system, although the differences are of emphasis rather than substance. The figure of Abhinavagupta is central to the exposition. A chapter is devoted to the poets of Kashmiri Shaivism. A final section draws parallels between Shaivite and Christian mysticism.

316 Sufism in Kashmīr from the fourteenth to the sixteenth century.

Abdul Qaiyum Rafiqi.   Varanasi, India; Delhi: Bharatiya Publishing House, c. 1978. 310p. map. bibliog.

A scholarly study based on extensive use of Persian sources. Although Sufism has been recognized as a major component of the Islamic tradition in Kashmir, this is one of the few critical studies of the subject. Rafiqi succeeds in giving a connected account of the role of the Sufi orders in the period when Islam was becoming fully established in the region. He pays special attention to the indigenous order of Rishis, which had its roots in pre-Islamic religious practice and whose principal figure was Sheikh Nuruddin. More general works on Sufism include *A history of Sufism in India*, by Saiyid Athar Abbas Rizvi (Delhi: Munshiram Manoharlal, 1978, 1983. 2 vols. - vol. 1, *Early Sufism and its history in India to 1600 AD*, vol. 2, *From sixteenth century to modern century*); and *The Sufi orders in Islam* by J. Spencer Trimingham (Oxford: Clarendon Press, 1971).

317 Purity and power among the Brahmans of Kashmir.

Alexis Sanderson.   In: *The category of the person*.   Edited by Michael Carrithers, Steven Collins, Steven Lukes.   Cambridge, England: Cambridge University Press, 1985, p. 190-216. bibliog.

Using mediaeval Sanskrit texts, Sanderson discusses the various philosophical views then prevalent in Kashmir on the relationship of the individual person to the universal. He concludes that there was a highly sophisticated debate at the time on such questions as consciousness and agency. His analysis relates to the region's Shaivite and tantric traditions.

318 The philosophy of sādhanā with special reference to the Trika philosophy of Kashmir.
Deba Brata SenSharma.   Albany, New York: State University of New York Press, 1990. Rev. ed. (SUNY series in Tantric studies, vol. 3).

SenSharma sets out the main doctrines of Kashmiri Shaivism and then discusses the way to self-realization and liberation (*jivanmukti*) through divine grace by means of the tantric practices collectively described as *sadhana*, or spiritual discipline. The study was first published in 1983.

319 The word of Lalla the prophetess.
Translated by Richard Carnac Temple.   Cambridge, England: Cambridge University Press, 1924. 292p.

Lal Ded, or Lalla Yogishwari, was a 14th-century mystic whose poems have exerted a great influence on popular religious consciousness in Kashmir. She came from the Shaivite tradition of the region, but was influenced by other religious currents, including Sufism. Her poems are expressions of her religious beliefs and strivings towards identification with the universal self. Temple's free translation of the poems is preceded by an extensive introduction to Lal Ded's own religious thought and the background to it. Temple's more popular work was closely based on the scholarly edition of Lal Ded's poems by George Grierson and Lionel D. Barnett, *Lalla Vakyani or the wise sayings of Lal Ded, a mystic poetess of ancient Kashmir* (London: The Royal Asiatic Society, 1920 [Asiatic Society Monographs, vol. 17]). This includes extensive discussion of the linguistic as well as the philosophical aspects of her poetry. A more recent study of Lal Ded is by Jayalal Kaul, *Lal Ded* (Delhi: Sahitya Akademi, 1973).

Social Structure

320 The angel of death in disguise: a North Indian case study.
Sangeeta Chattoo. Nedlands, Western Australia: University of
Western Australia, 1992. 35p. bibliog. (Centre for Asian Studies,
Occasional Paper, no. 4).
Extracted from a doctoral thesis, this is a sensitive study of how Muslims in the Kashmir
valley make sense of illness and death in terms of their religious beliefs. As in most other
cultures, there is a distinction between timely and untimely death, and a sense that
suffering has a redemptive purpose.

**321 Zentrale Gewalt in Nager (Karakorum): politische
Organisationsformen, ideologische Begründungen des
Königtums und Veränderungen in der Moderne.** (Centralized
power in Nager [Karakorum]: forms of political organization and
ideological foundations of kingship and transformations in the
modern period.)
Jürgen Frembgen. Wiesbaden, Germany: Franz Steiner Verlag,
1985. 241p. maps. bibliog. (Beiträge zur Südasienforschung,
Südasien-Institut Universität Heidelberg, no. 103).
This is a work of political anthropology which discusses state forms in the Karakoram
region in the northern mountains and in particular the kingdom that existed in Nager for
several centuries until its absorption into Pakistan in 1972. Frembgen discusses the
segmentary and unitary elements within the state.

322 An anthropological bibliography of South Asia.
Compiled by Elizabeth von Fürer-Haimendorf, Helen Kanitkar.
The Hague, Paris: Mouton, 1958-76. 4 vols.
This major work has a complicated history as well as internal organization of material.
The first two volumes, published in 1958 and 1964 and covering between them the period

up to 1959, were compiled by Elizabeth von Fürer-Haimendorf; the third, which appeared in 1970 and went up to 1964, was a joint effort between von Fürer-Haimendorf and Helen Kanitkar; and the fourth, which appeared in 1976 and covered the period up to 1969, was primarily compiled by Kanitkar. As well as the bibliographical references, each volume included a list of work in progress. The work includes many references for the Kashmir region, relating not only to social structure but also to folk culture and economic conditions. Some additional references on the position of women can be found in *Women of South Asia: a guide to resources*, compiled by Carol Sakala (Millwood, New York: Kraus International Publications, 1980).

323 Family and kinship: a study of the Pandits of rural Kashmir.
T. N. Madan.   Delhi: Oxford University Press, 1989. 2nd ed. 325p. map. bibliog.

First published in 1965 by Asia Publishing House, this is an important anthropological study of the Kashmiri Pandit community (to which Madan himself belongs), and is based on intensive fieldwork done in the village of Utrassu-Umanagri, near Anantnag, in 1958. Most of the book is an analysis of data collected on family and household structure, although there is a preliminary section on the Pandit community as a whole. Madan emphasizes the central role of the *chulah*, or household, organized around related male members. Appendices list kinship terminology in Kashmiri, and a number of Kashmiri proverbs illustrating family dynamics. There is also a new introduction that reviews the reception of the book and progress in the field since the first edition, and an additional appendix that offers personal reflections on the experience of fieldwork in the village – 'living intimately with strangers', as Madan terms it. Another book by Madan which draws extensively on his work on the Kashmiri Pandits and relates it to themes such as domesticity, good conduct and the goals of life, and the significance of death is *Non-renunciation: themes and interpretations of Hindu culture* (Delhi: Oxford University Press, 1987).

324 Muslim communities of South Asia: culture, society and power.
Edited by T. N. Madan.   Delhi: Manohar, 1995. 544p.

This is a revised and enlarged edition of a work first published in 1973 as a special issue of *Contributions to Indian Sociology* and then as a book (Delhi: Vikas) in 1976. Kashmir is featured in two articles. The first is by the editor and is entitled 'The social construction of cultural identities in rural Kashmir', in which Madan argues, based on his field work in a village in Anantnag (see previous entry), that the Muslim population operates with a dual set of representations of themselves and of their Hindu neighbours, one drawn from ideology (i.e. Islam) and the other from 'the compulsions of daily living', based on economic interdependence. As many other writers have also noted, Muslim society in South Asia contains many different groups, often divided along occupational lines. The second article (not included in the original edition), by Aparna Rao, is a study of social groupings among the Bakkarwal, who are nomadic goat breeders.

325 The Ladakhi: a study in ethnography and change.
R. S. Mann.   Calcutta, India: Anthropological Survey of India, 1986. 181p. bibliog.

Based on fieldwork carried out at the beginning of the 1970s, this reviews the social structure of the Ladakhi population, covering such standard ethnographic topics as marriage, family structure, and birth and death rituals, as well as traditional economic and political structures.

326 Astor: eine Ethnographie. (Astor: an ethnography.)
Adam Nayyar. Wiesbaden, Germany: Franz Steiner Verlag, 1986. 120p. map. bibliog. (Beiträge zur Südasienforschung, Südasien-Institut Universität Heidelberg, no. 88).

Astor is a valley settlement on the northern side of Nanga Parbat in the Northern Areas. Nayyar's account of the people that live there concentrates on their traditional world-view and religious practices, especially the role of the *shaman*. He also discusses the recent impact of Islam on the region. Appendices give the text and German translations of representative *shaman* and lineage songs.

327 Autonomy: life cycle, gender and status among Himalayan pastoralists.
Aparna Rao. New York, Oxford: Berghahn Books, 1998. 350p. bibliog.

The author is a professional anthropologist, and this substantial study addresses itself to the question of how individuals are able to assert their individuality while remaining embedded within their communities and traditions. The empirical focus of the study are the Bakkarwal, nomadic pastoralists who move with their flocks between winter and summer pastures within Jammu and Kashmir, and the book contains much very detailed information about life cycles and rituals.

328 The Balti: a scheduled tribe of Jammu and Kashmir.
B. R. Rizvi. Delhi: Gyan Publishing House, 1993. 123p. bibliog.

This is a standard ethnographical study of the Balti, the tribe which gives Baltistan its name. Shia by religion, the author sees them as marginalized by all their neighbours. He has based his study, conducted in the mid-1970s, on two villages in the Kargil area, one of which is very near the line of control.

329 The boats and the boatmen of Kashmir.
Shanta Sanyal. Delhi: Sagar Publications, 1979. 115p. bibliog.

A brief ethnography of the families who own and run the famous houseboats and *shikaras* (small boats) of Srinagar. The author examines many different aspects of their lives, from family and marriage patterns to problems such as indebtedness and poor health facilities. There is also some information about the boats themselves.

330 The Kashmiri Pandits: a study of cultural choice in north India.
Henny Sender. Delhi: Oxford University Press, 1988. 324p. bibliog.

From at least the 17th century onwards, members of the Kashmiri Pandit community sought their fortune on the plains of north India, first at the Mughal courts and later under the British. Jawaharlal Nehru came from such a family, as did many other distinguished lawyers and civil servants. The community maintained a strong cohesion while adopting many elements of the Urdu and Persian court culture of the period. Sender's study, originally a PhD thesis from the University of Wisconsin, traces in careful detail the history of the Kashmiri Pandit diaspora up to 1930. He sees them as brokers between the ruling groups and broader Hindu society. As a highly literate and socially conscious group, the Kashmiri Pandits were among the first to discuss and implement social reform in areas such as foreign travel, and Sender discusses these issues in detail. A similar and equally valuable study of the Pandits of north India is by Kusum Pant, *The Kashmiri Pandit: story of a community in exile in the nineteenth and twentieth centuries* (Delhi: Allied Publishers, 1987). Sender also contributed a detailed chapter, 'Kashmiri Pandits and their changing role in the culture of Delhi', covering the period from the early 17th century to 1857, in a collective volume edited by Robert Frykenberg, *Delhi through the ages: essays in urban history, culture and society* (Delhi: Oxford University Press, 1986).

331 Ethnologie und Geschichte: Festschrift für Karl Jettmar.
(Ethnology and history: *Festschrift* for Karl Jettmar.)
Edited by Peter Snoy. Wiesbaden, Germany: Franz Steiner Verlag, 1983. 654p. maps. bibliog. (Beiträge zur Südasien-Forschung, Südasien-Institut Universität Heidelberg, no. 86).

This *Festschrift* in honour of the leading foreign scholar of the Northern Areas includes contributions from fifty-six scholars from across the world. Most are written in German but there are some in English and a couple in French. For the most part they are in the fields of archaeology, ethnology and history, and relate both to the Northern Areas and to Afghanistan.

332 Ein Labyrinth von Identitäten in Nordpakistan: zwischen Landbesitz, Religion und Kaschmir-Konflikt. (A labyrinth of identities in North Pakistan: between landholding, religion and the Kashmir conflict.)
Martin Sökefeld. Cologne, Germany: Rüdiger Köppe Verlag, 1997. 383p. maps. bibliog. (Culture Area Karakorum Scientific Studies, vol. 8).

Originally a thesis, this is a theoretically oriented analysis of the various social and political identities to be found in the town of Gilgit. The discussion focuses on distinctions that people in the town make between Gilgit people and outsiders and between Sunni and Shia groups, and how these distinctions themselves have evolved in the last few years. There is also a chapter on the emergence of local political organizations, in particular the Balawaristan National Front, attempting to represent the interests of the Northern Areas as a whole and demanding local autonomy. There is a brief English summary.

Social Change and Social Problems

333 Daughters of the Vitasta: a history of Kashmiri women from early times to the present day.
Prem Nath Bazaz.   Delhi: Pamposh Publications, 1959. 279p. bibliog.

A popular account of the subject. The author gives vignettes of individual women such as the famous poetess Lalla (Lal Ded) and female rulers. There is a brief account of the 19th and 20th centuries.

334 Education, population and development: a regional perspective of Northwest India (Jammu and Kashmir, Punjab, Himachal Pradesh, Haryana and Rajasthan).
Y. P. Chaithley.   Chandigarh, India: Centre for Research in Rural and Industrial Development, 1995. 570p. bibliog. maps.

This substantial piece of research is based on a wide range of government and semi-government statistics and surveys, including often difficult to obtain material on education, as well as field studies conducted in 1989 and 1990. As far as possible, data is disaggregated down to *tehsil* level, that is, to units of often no more than 200,000 in population. As the title suggests, the purpose of the work is to investigate interrelationships between education, demographic factors and social and economic development, for example by looking at factors such as female literacy, although broader conclusions are to some extent submerged by the sheer volume of data.

335 Working women in Kashmir.
Bashir A. Dabla.   Jaipur, India: Rawat Publications, 1991. 124p. bibliog.

Based on work carried out in 1986 to 1988, the aim of this book is to look at changing attitudes and behaviour among Kashmiri women, with special emphasis on women working outside the home.

336 Tourismus in Hunza: Beziehungen zwischen Gästern und Gastgebern. (Tourism in Hunza: relations between guests and hosts.)
Jürgen Frembgen. *Sociologus* (N.S.), vol. 33, no. 2 (1983), p. 174-85.

Hunza, in the Northern Areas, is seen by many as a 'shangri-la' and has attracted many tourists in recent years. In the spirit of recent anthropological questioning of the impact of tourism on hitherto remote groups, the author looks at the negative effects in Hunza on the integrity of local cultural patterns.

337 Education and development.
B. L. Raina. Ambala, India: Indian Publications, 1992. 252p. bibliog.

Originally a thesis, the author uses a detailed case study of a village in Kashmir to illustrate his general argument about the connection between educational provision and local economic development. A mixed picture of the situation in the village emerges from the study.

338 Child labour in India.
Nazir Ahmad Shah. Delhi: Anmol Publications, 1992. 143p. bibliog.

Despite the title, this is entirely about the extent and conditions of child labour in Kashmir. The author looks in particular at child workers in carpet weaving, handicrafts, domestic service and restaurants, and has collected his data through interviews with employers, child employees, and parents. While identifying child labour as a major problem, he concludes that legal measures by themselves are unlikely to eliminate it. Given that the main cause for child labour is low family income among the poor, child labour can only be eliminated as part of a broader programme aimed at eliminating poverty. Further details of the abuse and exploitation of children employed in carpet weaving are given in a pamphlet written by Peter Cross, *Kashmiri carpet children: exploited village weavers* (London: Anti-Slavery International, Bulletin 2, 1991). Cross collected his data during two visits in 1989.

Constitutional and Legal System

339 The development of the constitution of Jammu and Kashmir.
Adarsh Sein Anand.   Delhi: Light and Life Publishers, 1980. 377p.
map. bibliog.
Originally a PhD thesis in the field of constitutional law, this study covers the
constitutional development of Jammu and Kashmir before as well as after independence.
As the author points out, the circumstances of the state's political history are such that it
is unique within India in being governed by two constitutional documents, although the
two fit together in such a way as to avoid the possibility of a clash of jurisdiction at the
constitutional level. The work deals separately with the position of the state under the
Indian constitution and with the constitution adopted by the state itself in 1957.

340 Kashmir – retrospect and prospect.
P. B. Gajendragadkar.   Bombay, India: University of Bombay, 1967.
147p. bibliog.
These three lectures were delivered in 1966 by a distinguished lawyer and judge. He
reviews the legal basis of the dispute and pronounces that Kashmir's accession to India is
'valid, final and irrevocable', and that Pakistan has forfeited any rights it had through its
actions after 1947. He also insists on the longstanding Indian position that to allow a
plebiscite would be to open up a Pandora's box of communal hatreds.

341 Jammu & Kashmir law reporter.
Jammu and Srinagar, India: High Court of Jammu & Kashmir. 1970- .
The official publication of the High Court in Indian Kashmir, this is produced monthly
but with continuous pagination for each year. Its main contents are the judgements of the
court in important cases. Indexes provide guidance to the points in dispute and the
relevant legislation considered. A similar, although unofficial, publication is the *Kashmir
law journal* (Jammu, India: the Editors, 1962-), which has been published for longer.
Many, but not all, cases are reported in both places.

342 Panchayati raj in Jammu and Kashmir.
Edited by George Mathew. Delhi: Concept, 1990. 165p.

The Indian system of elected local government, introduced in 1959, is known as *panchayati raj*, after the traditional institution of the *panchayat*, or group of five elders. *Panchayati raj* is seen as having both developmental and political goals. The essays included in this volume were presented at a seminar in Srinagar as part of the process of introducing new *panchayati raj* legislation in 1989. Although in the short term the legislation was overtaken by the outbreak of the insurgency, the papers contain valuable insights on how local government should be organized in the state. The text of the legislation is included as an appendix.

343 A textbook on Muslim personal law.
David Pearl. London, Sydney, Wolfeboro, New Hampshire: Croom Helm, 1987. 2nd ed. 284p. bibliog.

First published in 1979, this is intended primarily for the specialist but is accessible to others interested in family law among Muslims. Pearl places special emphasis on Muslims of the Indian subcontinent and refers frequently to law cases from India and Pakistan. Since 1977, Muslims in Jammu and Kashmir have been brought under the scope of Islamic law in so far as it applies to family matters, and to the extent that it has not been overridden by other legislation. This puts them on a par with Muslims in the rest of India, to whom the Sharia (Muslim law code) has applied since 1937.

344 Jammu and Kashmir: political and constitutional development.
Jaswant Singh. Delhi: Har-Anand Publications, 1996. 375p.

The author is a distinguished lawyer who served as chief justice of Jammu and Kashmir in the 1970s. The work consists of a brief introduction, followed by selected constitutional documents relating both to the pre- and post-1947 periods. These amplify, for example, the question of 'state subject' status, and include the text of the 1957 constitution of Jammu and Kashmir on the basis of its special status within the Indian Union.

345 Kashmir's special status.
Krishna Mohan Teng, Santosh Kaul. Delhi: Oriental Publishers, 1975. 244p. bibliog.

This is a scholarly account of the changing constitutional position of Jammu and Kashmir since 1948, especially around the time of the Delhi Agreement of 1952, which allowed for the state's closer integration into India. The authors make the point that the existence of article 370, under which the state continues to enjoy a somewhat distinct status within India, does not affect India's sovereignty. They also clearly believe that the state's special status is a historical hangover and that only with full integration into the Indian Union would healthy economic and social development be possible.

Armed Forces

346 The Frontier Scouts.
Charles Chenevix Trench.   London: Jonathan Cape, 1985. 298p.
maps. bibliog.

The Frontier Corps was a major example of the classic British technique of dealing with 'unruly' tribesmen. Selected locals were recruited into special units, and were then expected to keep the peace in the area concerned. The corps included the Gilgit Scouts, raised in 1913, who played a key role, under the command of Major William Brown, in the mini *coup d'état* in Gilgit which followed the Maharaja's accession to India in 1947. The latter's political agent, Brigadier Ghansar Singh, was detained while Brown declared that the state had acceded to Pakistan. Trench gives a detailed account of events, as well as a brief note on the way Gilgit and its neighbouring states were administered during the British period. Brown's diary has been published as *The Gilgit rebellion 1947* (Ibex, 1998). Another relevant military history is Arthur J. Barker, *Townshend of Kut* (London: Cassell, 1967). Major-General Sir Charles Townshend served in the region as a young subaltern, and took part in the Hunza campaign of 1891.

347 Battle for Pakistan: the air war of 1965.
John Fricker.   Shepperton, England: Ian Allan, 1979. 192p. map.

A strictly military account by a British journalist and writer of the air war in September 1965. The author had full cooperation from the Pakistan Air Force and was therefore in a position to give a detailed narrative of the actions that were fought. A chapter is devoted to the operations undertaken to place infiltrators into Kashmir. The book is well illustrated by photographs.

348 The first round: Indo-Pakistan War 1965.
M. Asghar Khan, foreword by Altaf Gauhar.   London: Islamic Information Services, 1979. 146p.

The author was commander-in-chief of the Pakistan Air Force until July 1965, two months before the war, intended to achieve a *coup de main* in Kashmir, broke out, and was familiar with the diplomatic as well as military background. During the war itself he was active in obtaining military supplies from friendly countries such as China and Turkey. The book, written we are told in 1966-67, combines personal reminiscence with observations on the actions and decisions of the principal actors on the Pakistan side. He is critical of United States policy towards the combatants and of Ayub Khan for agreeing to a cease-fire rather than continuing the military action at a moment when he thinks a breakthrough might have been made. He remarks in the introduction that the war 'appears now to have been fought for no purpose'.

349 History of Jammu and Kashmir Rifles 1820-1956: the state force background.
K. Brahma Singh.   Delhi: Lancer International, 1990. 324p. maps. bibliog.

The Jammu and Kashmir Rifles, now part of the Indian army, had their origins in the Jammu state forces raised in the early 19th century. They served both on internal security duties and as part of the British imperial forces during the world wars, and then played a part in the 1947-48 fighting in the state. The author is a retired officer of the regiment, and his account follows the usual detailed pattern of regimental histories. Another military history of the state is by D. K. Palit, *Jammu and Kashmir arms* (Dehra Dun, India: Palit & Palit, 1972).

Economy

350 Evaluation of District Council Kotli Azad Jammu & Kashmir (1985-1990).
Aminullah, Muhammad Humayun, Saeedullah.   Peshawar,
Pakistan: Pakistan Academy for Rural Development, 1992. 169p.
bibliog.
The focus of this piece of research is the effectiveness of local councils in the northern
part of Azad Jammu and Kashmir in stimulating rural development. The general
conclusions are fairly negative.

351 Social implications of technological changes in rural Kashmir: a comparative study of two villages of Anantnag District in Kashmir.
Mohd. Aslam.   Delhi: Inter-India Publications, 1981. 147p. map.
bibliog.
Originally a PhD thesis, this work is based on a sample survey of farmers in two villages.
The two questions with which the author is primarily concerned are, on the one hand, the
factors (for example age, level of education) that lead some to adopt new farming
methods more rapidly than others, and, on the other, the subsequent impact of adoption
on life-styles and aspirations.

352 A socio-economic study of farming systems in Azad Jammu and Kashmir.
M. Jameel Khan, Muhammad Sarwar, Muhammad Akram.   Lahore,
Pakistan: Punjab Economic Research Institute, 1982. 155p.
(Publication no. 197).
This is a report of an applied research project on agriculture in Azad Jammu and Kashmir,
based largely on survey work carried out in 1980. The study provides extensive data on
topics such as cropping patterns, size of holding and extent of use of family labour. The
study also draws to some extent on an agricultural census carried out in 1972.

353 Poverty, planning and economic change in Jammu and Kashmir.
M. L. Misri, M. S. Bhat.   Delhi: Vikas Publishing House, 1994.
403p. bibliog.

This important study by two professional economists looks at the incidence of poverty in Jammu and Kashmir, and tries to relate this to economic structures and government interventions over the past several decades. Partly because of the political situation, there have in fact been more radical measures taken in Jammu and Kashmir than in many other parts of India, most notably in the area of land tenure, and the authors argue that these have had a beneficial effect on reducing the incidence of poverty, even though there are still many poor people, especially in the more remote areas.

354 Farmers of India. vol. 1. Punjab, Himachal Pradesh, Jammu and Kashmir.
Edited by M. S. Randhawa, Prem Nath.   Delhi: Indian Council of Agricultural Research, 1959. 302p. bibliog.

Based on a wide range of secondary sources, this is a useful if rather dated study of agriculture in India's various regions. Approximately seventy pages are devoted to Jammu and Kashmir, with notes on soil types, crops, and agricultural practices, as well as ethnographic material on different agricultural communities. The book includes a number of good black-and-white photographs.

355 Regional transport survey of Jammu and Kashmir.
New Delhi: National Council of Applied Economic Research, 1975.
220p.

Based on data collected in 1971, this officially commissioned piece of research reviews the transport provision in the region in the light of economic requirements. The work contains detailed analyses not only of transport facilities but also of trade patterns.

356 Export marketing of Kashmir handicrafts.
Manzoor Ahmed Shah.   Delhi: Ashish Publishing House, 1992.
214p. bibliog.

This is a policy-oriented work on the issue of how to improve the marketing of Kashmir's handicrafts, its major source of export earnings apart from tourism. The author includes extensive statistical information from government sources, as well as the results of a sample survey of Kashmiri handicraft exporters he carried out in the late 1980s.

357 Statistical abstract India.
Delhi: Government of India, Central Statistical Organisation, Department of Statistics. Annual.

This basic source for all aspects of India's economy covers Jammu and Kashmir, although the data for the state on some topics is clearly very patchy.

Literature

358 The way of the swan: poems of Kashmir.
Nilla Cram Cook.   Bombay, India: Asia Publishing House, 1958.
148p.
After a substantial introduction that emphasizes the religious and spiritual background to Kashmiri poetry, the author collects and translates a representative collection from Lal Ded (from one of whose poems the book's title is taken) to 20th-century poets.

359 Masterpieces of Indian literature.
Edited by K. M. George.   Delhi: National Book Trust, 1997. 3 vols.
Published by the official National Book Trust to mark India's golden jubilee, volume one contains a section edited by Shashi Shekhar Toshkhani and devoted to brief studies of fourteen major works in Kashmiri from Lal Ded in the 14th century to Mahjoor in the 20th century.

360 Kingfishers catch fire.
Rumer Godden.   London: Pan, 1966. 253p.
First published in 1953, this partly autobiographical novel by the well-known writer Rumer Godden, herself born and brought up in India, is set in pre-1947 Kashmir, where she spent three years. The main protagonist, a young Englishwoman recently widowed, brings her children to a remote Kashmiri village. Her attempts to get close to the villagers are misunderstood and end in tragedy. A collection of short stories by Rumer Godden and her sister Jon, *Indian dust: stories by Rumer and Jon Godden* (London: Macmillan, 1989), includes several set in Kashmir. A biography of Rumer Godden by Anne Chisholm, *Rumer Godden: a storyteller's life* (London: Macmillan, 1998), indicates the autobiographical element.

361 Kashmiri literature.
Braj B. Kachru. Wiesbaden, Germany: Otto Harrassowitz, 1981.
114p. bibliog. (A History of Indian Literature, vol. 8, fascicle 4).

A scholarly review of the subject which starts from the 14th century and comes up to the present. Within a limited space, Kachru is able to cover linguistic and stylistic topics, as well as the religious and political background to various writers. Other fascicles in the History of Indian Literature Series also contain references to Kashmir, for example volume 7, Annemarie Schimmel, *Islamic literatures of India* (1973) and volume 3, fascicle 1, Siegfried Lienhard, *A history of classical poetry: Sanskrit – Pali – Prakrit* (1984).

362 Studies in Kashmiri.
Jayalal (J. L.) Kaul. Srinagar, India: Kapoor Brothers, 1968. 339p.

This is, in effect, a history of Kashmiri literature by an eminent scholar of the subject. There are thematic chapters on aspects of prose and poetry, and chapters devoted to the poetry of Lal Ded, Haba Khatoon, Arnimaal, Paramanand and Zinda Kaul. Each chapter is illustrated with extensive translations. Two closely related works by Kaul are *Kashmiri lyrics* (Srinagar, India: Rinemisray, 1945) and *Kashmiri literature* (Mysore, India: Prasaranga, 1970).

363 Gems of Kashmiri literature.
Edited by T. N. Kaul. Delhi: Sanchar Publishing House, 1996.
243p.

This is a collection of prose and poetry translations by various hands, assembled by a retired Kashmiri journalist (not to be confused with the diplomat of the same name), which provides an overview of the subject from medieval mystics such as Lal Ded to 20th-century poets such as Mahjoor. There is a brief biographical note and appreciation for each writer, and for each poem (but not piece of prose) there is a romanized Kashmiri text alongside the translation.

364 Rasul Mir.
G. R. Malik. Delhi: Sahitya Akademi, 1990. 55p. bibliog.

Part of the Makers of Indian Literature series published by a semi-official institution, this is a succinct account of the 19th-century Kashmiri poet Rasul Mir, known for his romantic lyrics written in *ghazal* and *vatsun* forms. The author notes the strong Persian influence on form and imagery alike, and includes some translated examples.

365 The stranger beside me.
Edited and translated by Neerja Mattoo. Delhi: UBSPD, 1994.
152p.

This volume brings together fifteen short stories all originally in Kashmiri and written by authors born between 1926 and 1974. The editor provides an introduction that gives a brief history of Kashmiri literature and then introduces the stories themselves.

366 Contribution of Kashmir to Sanskrit literature.
K. S. Nagarajan. Bangalore, India: the author, 1970. 729p. map.
bibliog.

Originally a PhD thesis, this densely detailed work is most useful as a listing of Kashmiri writers in Sanskrit, including poets, historians and philosophers. There are extensive but untranslated extracts from their works.

367 An anthology of modern Kashmiri verse (1930-1960).
Selected and translated by Trilokinath Raina. Poona, India: Suresh Raina, 1972. 280p.

Seventeen poets altogether are represented in this anthology, including Mahjoor, Dina Nath Nadim and Abdul Ahad Azad. The translator contributes a critical introduction that discusses their changing concerns from the revolutionary zeal of the early period to the search for new forms of expression and idiom in the post-1947 period. There are brief biographical notes on each poet.

368 History of Dogri literature.
Shivanath. Delhi: Sahitya Akademi, 1976. 194p.

Although not recognized as one of India's main languages, Dogri has a distinct identity as the local language of the Jammu region. Shivanath's history covers folk literature, before discussing in more detail the emergence of Dogri literature in various genres from the 1940s on. Dr Karan Singh, the last Maharaja of the state, has himself written Dogri poetry and has brought together a collection of traditional songs, *Shadow and sunlight: an anthology of Dogra-Pahari songs* (London: Asia Publishing House, 1962). For each song, there is the original text, English and Hindi translations, and musical annotations.

369 Persian literature: a bio-bibliographical survey. Section II, fasc. 3.
C. A. Storey. London: Luzac, 1939, p. 433-780.

This comprehensive survey of manuscripts in Persian includes a section on Kashmir, Jammu and Hunza. Each entry contains biographical notes on the author, a brief annotation and bibliographical details, including a note of location and of any published version. The Persian sources for the Mughal Empire are also listed. The fascicle forms part of the first volume of the survey, which was eventually published in 1970 (London: Royal Asiatic Society).

The Arts

General

370   Marg. vol. 8, no. 2 (March 1955).
Edited by Mulk Raj Anand. 159p. bibliog. map. (Special issue on Kashmir).

This special issue of India's premier popular arts magazine carries articles on many different aspects of the arts and literature of Kashmir. There are four feature articles by well-known scholars – by Percy Brown on the Hindu and Buddhist architecture of Kashmir, by Charles Fabri on terracottas, by H. Goetz on mediaeval sculpture, and by J. R. Nichols on Muslim architecture – together with an extract from John Irwin's book on shawls. These are accompanied by briefer pieces on crafts, music, contemporary art and literature and also by photographs, sketches and poems. Finally, there is a useful chronology of the region from the earliest times until 1947, covering the arts as well as politics.

371   Marg. vol. 40, no. 2 (March 1989).
Edited by Pratapaditya Pal. 79p. (Special issue on Kashmir).

Another special issue, but more conventional in format. Pride of place goes to three articles by Robert E. Fisher, two on early Buddhist architecture, including a detailed account of the monastic ruins at Harwan, and one on early stone temples. The article on Harwan suggests that the site was originally occupied by a Hindu ascetic sect, the Ajivikas, whose presence in Kashmir is otherwise unrecorded. The other two articles are by John Siudmak on early stone and terracotta sculpture, and by the editor on Kashmir's links with Tibet, based on the evidence of bronze sculptures.

Visual arts

372 Miniatures from Kashmirian manuscripts.
Adel Adamova, T. Greck.   Leningrad: Iskusstvo, 1976. 237p.

This work is based on a number of illuminated Persian manuscripts in Leningrad libraries, which the authors argue are of Kashmiri origin, dating from the 18th and early 19th centuries. Their arguments in favour of this provenance are based partly on textual and partly on stylistic grounds. The book includes many reproductions of miniatures, although the quality of these is not good.

373 The Kashmir shawl: and its Indo-French influence.
Frank Ames.   Woodbridge, England: Antique Collectors Club, 1988. rev. ed. 347p. map. bibliog.

Designed for the enthusiastic and knowledgeable amateur, the first part of this book presents a history of shawls and shawl-making, and a study of the motifs used. The second presents a detailed guide, lavishly illustrated with colour and black-and-white plates, to patterns used from the 17th to the 19th centuries. The author also covers the interest taken in Kashmir shawls in Europe in this period, especially in France. Another important study of Kashmir shawls, which focuses on the interaction between India and Europe, is by John Irwin: *Shawls* (London: Victoria and Albert Museum, 1955).

374 Architecture of Mughal India.
Catherine B. Asher.   Cambridge, England: Cambridge University Press, 1992. 368p. map. bibliog. (New Cambridge History of India, volume 1 part 4).

As part of the *New Cambridge History of India*, this volume provides a careful overview of the latest research on the subject of Mughal architecture and presents it in an accessible form. It is useful both for the background information it provides on Mughal architectural styles and for the specific references to buildings in Kashmir and their social functions.

375 Painted wooden covers of two Gilgit manuscripts in the Sri Pratap Museum, Srinagar (Jammu and Kashmir).
P. Banerjee.   *Oriental Art*, vol. 14, no. 2 (Summer 1968), p. 114-18.

The two manuscripts that are the focus of this study were discovered in 1938. The painted covers, well reproduced here, show images of the Buddha and of Boddhisattvas. Banerjee dates them to the 9th century, and argues that stylistically they demonstrate the region's contact with Central Asia. They are, he says, the earliest known examples of Kashmiri painting.

376 Jammu ragamala paintings.
Sukhdev Singh Charak.   Delhi: Abhinav Publications, 1998. 80p.

Ragamala paintings are miniatures which portray the mood of the various musical modes or ragas. They are recorded in the Jammu region from the late 17th century. This work concentrates on the style and iconography of two 19th-century series of paintings, which were until recently housed in a Jammu temple but which are now lost. There are extensive colour and black-and-white illustrations.

377 Pahari styles of Indian murals.
Sukh Dev Singh Charak, Anita K. Billiwaria.   Delhi: Abhinav
Publications, 1998. bibliog. 156p.

After a discussion of wall-painting techniques and styles, the authors give a detailed account of many of the murals to be found in temples and palaces in Jammu and adjacent areas. Most of the paintings are of gods or of scenes from religious epics. There are many illustrative plates, some in colour but the majority in black and white.

378 The gardens of Mughul India: a history and guide.
Sylvia Crowe, Sheila Haywood, Susan Jellicoe, Gordon Patterson.
London: Thames & Hudson, 1972. 200p. maps. bibliog.

The formal gardens laid out by the Mughal rulers of India, with their interweaving of water, trees and flowers, have always attracted attention. The present work is designed for a generally interested audience but is carefully documented and illustrated, with extensive quotes from the memoirs of the Mughal emperors and from European travellers. There are many photographs and copies of miniatures, although most are in black and white. Several of the most famous gardens are located in Kashmir. An earlier book on the same subject is Constance Mary Villiers-Stuart, *Gardens of the Great Mughals* (London: A. & C. Black, 1913).

379 Kashmiri painting: assimilation and diffusion; production and patronage.
Karuna Goswamy.   Shimla, India: Indian Institute of Advanced
Study; Delhi: Aryan Books International, 1998. 180p. bibliog.

Extensively illustrated with colour reproductions, this is a comprehensive account of the subject by a professional art historian. Paintings include manuscript illustrations as well as separate works of art. The aim of the book is to present Kashmiri painting in its own right and not simply as an appendage to the Persian tradition. There is therefore equal emphasis on Muslim and Hindu themes. The author argues that most art patrons in Kashmir were bourgeois rather than aristocratic.

380 The art and architecture of the Indian subcontinent.
J. C. Harle.   Harmondsworth, England: Penguin Books, 1986. 597p.
maps. bibliog. (Pelican History of Art).

This comprehensive work on the subject of art and architecture in India includes a well-illustrated chapter on Kashmir, focusing mainly on temples and sculpture. There are brief references to Kashmir in the sections on painting.

381 Ancient monuments of Kashmir.
Ram Chandra Kak.   London: Indian Society, 1933. 172p. bibliog.

The author, who had been in charge of the state's archaeological department, offers a guide to its major monuments, written in a non-technical style and illustrated with plans and black-and-white photographs. There is an introductory section dealing with the region's history and with the main architectural styles to be found. Kak also wrote *Handbook of the archaeological and numismatic sections of the Sri Pratap Singh Museum, Srinagar* (Calcutta, India: Thacker, Spink & Co, 1923). This describes the sculptural and other highlights of the collection, but has very indifferent black-and-white plates.

382 Kashmir: Hindu, Buddhist and Muslim Architecture.
Manohar Kaul.   Delhi: Sagar Publications, 1971. 139p.

An introduction for the non-specialist to the pre-modern buildings of Kashmir. The author divides his material into three sections – ancient monuments (Buddhist and Hindu), Mughal garden buildings, and mosques and mausolea. For each building or group of buildings there is an architectural description, accompanied by a photograph, usually in black and white.

383 Mughal and other Indian paintings from the Chester Beatty Library.
Linda York Leach.   London: Scorpion Cavendish, 1995. 2 vols.

The main focus of this set is miniatures and manuscript illustrations produced during the Mughal and post-Mughal period. Kashmiri artists are covered as part of a chapter in the second volume. Each picture, reproduced either in colour or in black and white, is the subject of a careful stylistic analysis. Linda Leach also contributed a chapter on 'Painting in Kashmir from 1600 to 1650' to *Facets of Indian art*, edited by Robert Skelton (London: Victoria & Albert Museum, 1986), in which she argues that during this period Kashmiri painters were essentially dependent on the styles set elsewhere in the Mughal world. Mughal miniatures as a genre are the subject of a vast literature. Of particular interest in the context of Kashmir is *The emperors' album: images of Mughal India* by Stuart Cary Welch, Annemarie Schimmel, Marie L. Swietochowski and Wheeler M. Thackston (New York: Metropolitan Museum of Art, 1987), which focuses on a collection of miniatures painted for the emperors Jahangir and Shah Jahan. Jahangir was a particular devotee of the region.

384 Muhammadan architecture in Kashmir.
W. H. Nicholls.   Archaeological Survey of India, annual report 1906-07, p. 161-70.

Probably the earliest attempt at a systematic classification of styles of Muslim architecture in Kashmir. The main focus of attention is the region's distinctive wooden mosques, for example the Jama Masjid and the mosque of Shah Hamadan in Srinagar. The descriptions in the text are carefully and extensively illustrated.

385 Bronzes of Kashmir.
Pratapaditya Pal.   Graz, Vienna: Akademische Druck-u.Verlagsanstalt, 1975. 255p. bibliog.

The rich tradition of bronze statues and figures in Kashmir only came to the notice of the wider world in the 1950s. Pratapaditya Pal, the distinguished Indian art historian and museum curator, here provides a brief introduction to the bronzes, together with detailed notes on the 103 black-and-white plates of items dating from the 6th to 12th centuries. The majority are of Buddhist origin, although some are Hindu. A few of the items are from neighbouring areas such as Gandhara, and are included for comparative purposes.

386 **Early sculpture of Kashmir (before the middle of the eigth [sic] century A. D.). An approach to art history and epigraphy of the Jhelum valley and its peripheral regions.**
Pran Gopal Paul.   Leiden, The Netherlands: Sneldruk Enschede, 1986. 353p. map. bibliog.
This doctoral thesis sets out to establish the chronological development of sculpture in Kashmir in the early period. Only a very few dated images are available, so the argument is primarily on stylistic grounds. The author argues that by the end of the period under discussion, a distinct Kashmiri style of sculpture had emerged.

387 **Pre-Muhammadan monuments of Kashmir.**
Daya Ram Sahni.   Archaeological Survey of India, annual report 1915-16, p. 49-78.
The author was an official of the Archaeological Survey of India, a government department, who worked in Kashmir in 1913. This report provides a general account of Hindu and Buddhist architecture, and updates and revises the work of several earlier archaeologists, notably Alexander Cunningham and James Fergusson. The article is illustrated by a number of photographs and drawings.

388 **Dogra wall paintings in Jammu and Kashmir.**
Mira Seth.   Delhi: Oxford University Press, 1987. 59p. map. bibliog.
In the mid-19th century there was a vigorous tradition of wall painting in the small hill states of the Jammu region, both in domestic palaces and in temples. Influenced by the great Mughal tradition, the artists also drew on folk art to produce lively and brightly coloured illustrations, mostly of stories from Hindu mythology. The text is illustrated with 180 (unpaginated) colour and black-and-white photographs.

389 **The cultural heritage of Ladakh.**
David Snellgrove, Tadeusz Skorupski.   Warminister, England: Aris & Phillips, 1977, 1980. 2 vols. maps. bibliog. vol. 1 *Central Ladakh*; vol. 2 *Zangskar and the cave temples of Ladakh*.
This is a thorough introduction to the Buddhist temples of Ladakh by two distinguished Tibetologists. Extremely detailed, it is at the same time written in an accessible style and could be used to supplement conventional travel guides. The authors give personal accounts of their travels in Ladakh in the 1970s. Both volumes are extensively illustrated with black-and-white photographs of temples and murals. The second volume includes a translation of a Tibetan biography of Rin-chen bzang-po, the most important figure in the early history of Buddhism in Ladakh.

Music and dance

390 Thirty songs from the Panjab and Kashmir.
Recorded by Ratan Devi, introduction by Ananda K.
Coomaraswamy. London: the authors, 1913. 76p.

A typical private press production intended for a cultivated British audience, this
collaboration between an English woman (Ratan Devi) and the famed Indian critic
Ananda Coomaraswamy includes musical transcriptions of a number of songs from both
Kashmir and Jammu, as well as some interesting comments on the musical traditions of
the region.

391 Ṣūfyāna mūsīqī: the classical music of Kashmir.
Józef Pacholczyk. Berlin: Verlag für Wissenschaft und Bildung,
1996. 261p. map. bibliog. (Intercultural Music Studies 9)

The author, a professional ethnomusicologist, describes the Sufi music of the title,
originally performed especially by members of the *Qadiri* order, as belonging
traditionally to the urban elite of Kashmir, although it is now losing ground to other
musical forms. The book discusses all aspects of the music and its history, and traces its
connections with other musical forms in the Persian and Arab world. The book gives
musical transcriptions of several pieces, and there is an accompanying compact disc.

392 The new Grove dictionary of music and musicians.
Edited by Stanley Sadie. London: Macmillan, 1980. 20 vols. maps.
bibliog.

There is a comprehensive survey of South Asian music in volume 6 (p. 69-166), by
Harold S. Powers and others, which covers classical styles of music, as well as dance. In
volume 9 (p. 817-19), Powers discusses distinctively Kashmiri styles of music, especially
devotional music. There are brief entries in other volumes for performers, instruments and
styles. Extended entries for almost all the instruments used in South Asian music can be
found in *The new Grove dictionary of musical instruments*, edited by Stanley Sadie
(London: Macmillan, 1984. 3 vols.). A good introduction to North Indian classical music
is by N. A. Jairazbhoy, *The rāgs of north Indian music: their structure and evolution*
(Middletown, Connecticut: Wesleyan University Press, 1971).

Folklore and Festivals

393 Studies in Pakistani popular culture.
Edited by William L. Hanaway, Wilma Heston.   Lahore, Pakistan:
Sang-e-Meel Publications, Lok Virsa Publishing House, 1996. 615p.
maps. bibliog.

The specialist studies in this volume are the product of a joint Pakistani-American
research project in the late 1980s, looking at aspects of popular culture in Pakistan,
especially the Northern Areas. Three of the articles deal with those areas that fall within
the old Jammu and Kashmir boundaries. Margaret Mills writes on food and food customs
in a village in the Karakoram Mountains. Peter Edwin Hook takes as his theme local
versions of *Kesar*, a well-known Central Asian epic. Elena Bashir uses evidence from
languages such as Balti and Burushaski to contribute to the debate on the history of Indo-
Aryan languages and Dravidian influences on this process.

394 A bibliography of South Asian folklore.
Edwin Capers Kirkland.   Bloomington, Indiana: Indiana University,
1966. 291p. (Indiana University Folklore Series, no. 21; Asian
Folklore Studies Monographs, no. 4).

An unannotated but comprehensive and indexed listing of all types of material related to
South Asian folklore. There are numerous entries for Kashmir and several for the other
parts of the state.

395 A dictionary of Kashmiri proverbs and sayings.
J. Hinton Knowles.   Bombay, India: Education Society's Press,
1885. 263p.

This massive compilation of proverbs by a missionary and folklorist lists well over a
thousand proverbs arranged alphabetically. Each proverb is given in the original Kashmiri
(transcribed into roman) and then in translation. In most cases there is a brief gloss on the
meaning, and in a few cases a more extended illustration of its use in folk tales. Some of
the proverbs can be traced to Persian originals. The anthropologist T. N. Madan has
published a smaller collection of proverbs from the Kashmiri Pandit community on the

subject of kinship and family: 'Proverbs: the 'single-meaning' category', *Man*, vol. 63 (1963), p. 93. Omkar N. Koul's work, *A dictionary of Kashmiri proverbs* (Patiala, India: Indian Institute of Language Studies, 1992), is also useful.

396 Folk-tales of Kashmir.
J. Hinton Knowles.   London: Kegan Paul, Trench, Trübner & Co., 1893. 510p.

Knowles was a missionary who collected folk-tales in the late 19th century. After a brief introduction, the remainder of the volume is devoted to the recounting of some sixty stories from Kashmir, although as Knowles points out, many of them are variants on more widely spread stories. In each case he identifies the person who originally told him the story. The volume was reprinted in 1981 (Islamabad: National Institute of Folk Heritage). The volume by Bani Roy Chaudhury, *Folk Tales of Kashmir* (Delhi: Sterling Publishers, 1969) brings together twenty-five stories, told in the same style as Knowles.

397 Tawi tales: folk tales from Jammu.
Noriko Mayeda, W. Norman Brown.   New Haven, Connecticut: American Oriental Society, 1974. 609p. map. bibliog. (American Oriental Series, vol. 57).

This is both an important scholarly work and one that would interest the general reader. Brown taught in a college in Jammu in the early 1920s and took the opportunity to collect some eighty folk tales of the region. His PhD student, Noriko Mayeda, returned to the region forty years later to collect further stories and found that most of the early collection were still current. The work is in three parts. The first and briefest is a methodological and comparative study of folk tales, the second is the full text of Brown's collection translated into colloquial English, while the third provides a scholarly apparatus for each tale, identifying its basic motifs and mentioning parallel tales from other traditions.

Periodicals

398 Frontline.
Madras, India: Kasturi & Sons, 1984- . fortnightly.

This is one of a number of Indian weekly or fortnightly magazines to report regularly on Kashmir. Compared to most of its competitors, it specializes in longer, more analytical pieces, often from a left-wing perspective, for example those by Aijaz Ahmad on the Kargil crisis, published in July 1999. *India Today* should also be consulted. Both magazines are available online. *Frontline* is at www.frontlineonline.com; *India Today* is at www.india-today.com.

399 Viewpoint.
Lahore, Pakistan: Mazhar Ali Khan, 1975-92. weekly.

A distinctly unglossy and often rather idiosyncratic magazine that in its prime included some of the best critical journalism in Pakistan. A wide range of topics was covered in each issue, some oriented towards immediate events, others towards longer term issues. Its position on Kashmir, critical of the establishments of both India and Pakistan, reflected that of the secular intelligentsia. A somewhat similar position can be found more recently in the *Friday Times* (www.thefridaytimes.com), also published from Lahore.

Bibliographies

400 Bibliography of Asian Studies.
Ann Arbor, Michigan: Association for Asian Studies, 1941-91.
annual

Published until 1967 as a special issue of the *Journal of Asian Studies* (before 1956 *Far Eastern Quarterly*), this bibliography lists a wide range of European-language scholarly articles, reports and books on all aspects of Asian studies. Two cumulative versions of the earlier bibliographies, arranged both by author and by subject, have been published (Boston: G. K. Hall). These cover 1941-65 and 1966-70 respectively. South Asia was only included in the scope of the bibliography from 1955. The bibliography is now available electronically (only through library subscription). Coverage of the electronic version is being extended back to 1971, to ensure full continuity with the printed version. The bibliography is an essential tool for all interested in research on the humanities and social sciences related to Jammu and Kashmir.

401 A bibliography of Ladakh.
John Bray, with Nawang Tsering Shakspo.   Warminster, England:
Aris & Phillips, 1988. 153p.

Arranged alphabetically by author, this bibliography includes approximately 1,200 items on Ladakh, most with brief annotations. Many of the entries are in Tibetan. As the compiler says in his introduction, this is the only bibliography devoted exclusively to Ladakh, although geology and the natural sciences are excluded. It also includes recorded sound items. There is a subject index.

402 A select bibliography of periodical literature on India and Pakistan, 1947-70.
Compiled by Pervaiz Iqbal Cheema.   Islamabad: National
Commission on Historical and Cultural Research, 1976, 1979, 1984.
3 vols.

A compilation of over 5,000 entries from 575 journals covering an enormous range of topics, although there are no annotations. Subjects covered include cookery, sports, forestry, education and folktales, as well as the more common areas such as economics and foreign affairs. The journals that have been scanned include well-known academic periodicals but also a number of weekly and monthly popular magazines published in South Asia, the US and Britain. All sources are in English. The first volume deals with Pakistan, the second with India, and the third with both. Jammu and Kashmir is given its own section in the third volume, although there are relevant items in the first volume also. Additional guides to periodical literature, although they contain only limited numbers of items on the Kashmir region, have been edited by Margaret Case, *South Asian history, 1750-1950: a guide to periodicals, dissertations and newspapers* (Princeton, New Jersey: Princeton University Press, 1968); and by N. K. Goil, *Asian social science bibliography with annotations and abstracts* (Delhi: Hindustan Publishing Corporation (earlier Vikas), 1966-69).

403 Jammu and Kashmir: a selected and annotated bibliography of manuscripts, books and articles, together with a survey of its history, languages and literature from Rajatarangini to modern times.

Ramesh Chander Dogra.   Delhi: Ajanta Publications, 1986. 417p.

This *magnum opus* by a professional librarian brings together an extraordinary range of items, about three thousand altogether, on almost every aspect of Jammu and Kashmir in Indian and Western languages. It is particularly strong on articles published in periodicals originating from India, but also from Britain, the US and elsewhere. Even if history and politics are the most heavily covered topics, areas such as botany, folklore and technology are not neglected. Only a few of the items are in fact annotated, despite the title of the work. The items are classified by subject, and there are author and subject indexes. There are also lists of Persian and English manuscript sources and an extended factual introduction. A specialized bibliography that covers the Northern Areas is *Bibliography – Northern Pakistan*, edited by Irmtraud Stellrecht (Cologne, Germany: Rüdiger Köppe Verlag, 1998 [Culture Area Karakorum Scientific Studies, vol. 1]).

404 Theses on Indian sub-continent (1877-1971).

Compiled by Krishan Gopal, edited by Dhanpat Rai.   Delhi: Hindustan Publishing Corporation, 1977. 462p.

This work lists over 3,000 theses completed between 1877 and 1971 in North America, the British Isles and Australia. There is a subject index which guides the user to the entries related to the Kashmir region, although there is some duplication of entries. Selected dissertations are also listed by Case (see entry no. 402).

405 South Asian civilizations: a bibliographical synthesis.

Maureen L. P. Patterson, in collaboration with William J. Alspaugh. Chicago, London: University of Chicago Press, 1981. 853p. maps.

This monumental bibliography contains over 28,000 entries on all aspects of the subject. Although the entries are not annotated, the headings are well chosen to give as clear an insight as possible into the interconnections between the subjects covered. There is a section devoted to the Kashmir region and references in the thematic chapters as well.

406 Pakistan.
David Taylor.   Oxford; Santa Barbara, California; Denver,
Colorado: Clio Press, 1990. 255p. map. (World Bibliographical
Series, vol. 10)
In the same series as the present work, this contains entries relevant both to the Pakistan
side of the Indo-Pakistan dispute, as well as general background works on South Asia,
especially its Islamic traditions. The second edition of the parallel bibliography for India
(volume no. 26) was compiled by Ian Derbyshire (1995). The original edition was
compiled by Brijen K. Gupta and Datta S. Kharbas (1984). Neither contains many entries
of direct relevance to Kashmir.

**407 Jammu, Kashmir and Ladakh: a classified and comprehensive
bibliography.**
Kulbhushan Warikoo.   Delhi: Sterling, 1976. 555p.
This massive work contains 7,684 entries, exclusively in English and with very
occasional annotations. The majority of the entries are from journals and periodicals, and
the 20th-century history section includes many contemporary articles and short press
comments. In scope it is somewhat similar to the volume by R. C. Dogra, although the
latter is easier to use.

**408 A guide to Western manuscripts and documents in the British
Isles relating to South and South East Asia.**
Compiled by M. D. Wainwright, Noel Matthews.   London: Oxford
University Press, 1965. 532p.
This is a major research tool for anyone working on South Asia in the colonial period. It
lists in summary form the archival holdings of many different record offices and museums
in Britain, from the Public Record Office down to small regimental museums and
business firms. There is an extensive index by person and place, from which a number of
items relating to Kashmir, Jammu, Ladakh and the Northern Areas can be identified. The
records of the India Office Library and Records (well described in Martin Moir, *A general
guide to the India Office Library and Records* [London: British Library, 1988]) are
excluded, however.

Indexes

There follow three separate indexes: authors (personal or corporate); titles; and subjects. Title entries are italicized and refer either to the main titles, or to other works cited in the annotations. The numbers refer to bibliographical entry rather than page number. Individual index entries are arranged in alphabetical sequence.

Index of Authors

116

Index of Titles

119

121

123

124

128

130

Index of Subjects

Rasul Mir 364
Population
  age of marriage 273
  estimates 270
  history 271
  see also Censuses
Puri, Balraj 190

Q

Qasim, Mir 264

R

Rajatarangini 124
Religions 2
  Buddhism 13, 313, 389
  Christianity
    missionary activity 12,
      131, 268, 305, 310
  Hinduism *see* Religions:
    Shaivism; Religions:
    mysticism
  Islam 7, 303, 308
    Ahmadis 314
    beliefs about death 320
    Shi'ism 311
    sufism 125, 302-03,
      316
      Kubrawiyya 120
      music 391
  Ladakh 3, 11, 14
  mysticism 307
  Lal Ded 319
  Northern Areas 312, 326
  Shaivism 304, 306, 309,
    315, 317-18
Rin-chen bzang-po 389
Roja 204
Rushdie, Salman
  Satanic Verses 280

S

Sen, L. P. 166
Shah, Shabir 255
Shah Hamadan *see*
  Hamadani, Sayyid Ali
Shawls 10, 62, 370, 373
Shawl-weavers 143
Sheep *see* Flora and fauna
Shikaras *see* Boats
Singh, Dr Karan 266
Singh, Maharaja Gulab
  105, 131, 262, 265
Singh, Maharaja Hari 129,
  150, 259
Singh, Maharaja Pratap
  134, 138
Singh, Maharaja Ranbir
  253
Singh, Zorawar 104-05
Social change
  working women 335
Social problems
  child labour 338
Sports
  polo 24
Srinagar *see* History:
  Srinagar

T

Tourism
  impact on local
    population 13, 336
Travel 47
  bibliography 54
  guidebooks 72-75
  historical 55, 62, 70
  Kashmir 49, 69
    historical 45, 48, 51-52,
      56, 71
  Ladakh 43, 64

historical 53, 56, 62, 71
Northern Areas 44, 46,
  57-58, 61, 63, 65,
  68-69
Tyndale-Biscoe, C. E. 268
  see also Religions:
    Christianity:
    missionary activity

V

Vas, E. A. 167
Veterinary medicine 7

W

Wakhlu, Khem Lata 197
Wars
  1947-48 war 149, 157,
    164, 166-67, 349
  1962 Sino-Indian war
    196
  1965 war 176, 178, 236,
    239-40, 242, 347-48
  see also Armed forces
Wavell, Lord 160
Weights and measures 99
Wullar barrage 154

Y

Yearbooks
  Azad Kashmir 37
  Northern Areas 37
Younghusband, Francis 22,
  55

Z

Zanskar 15, 64, 74
  see also Ladakh

Map of Kashmir

This map shows the more important features. The boundaries marked are not drawn precisely to scale.

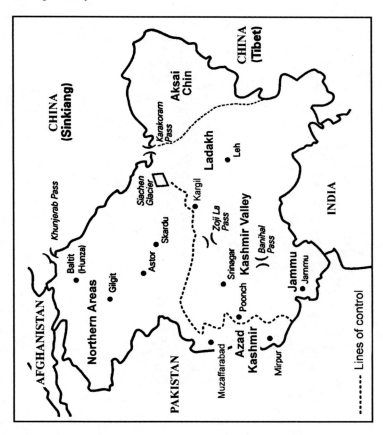

ALSO FROM CLIO PRESS

INTERNATIONAL ORGANIZATIONS SERIES

Each volume in the International Organizations Series is either devoted to one specific organization, or to a number of different organizations operating in a particular region, or engaged in a specific field of activity. The scope of the series is wide ranging and includes intergovernmental organizations, international non-governmental organizations, and national bodies dealing with international issues. The series is aimed mainly at the English-speaker and each volume provides a selective, annotated, critical bibliography of the organization, or organizations, concerned. The bibliographies cover books, articles, pamphlets, directories, databases and theses and, wherever possible, attention is focused on material about the organizations rather than on the organizations' own publications. Notwithstanding this, the most important official publications, and guides to those publications, will be included. The views expressed in individual volumes, however, are not necessarily those of the publishers.

VOLUMES IN THE SERIES

1 *European Communities*, John Paxton
2 *Arab Regional Organizations*, Frank A. Clements
3 *Comecon: The Rise and Fall of an International Socialist Organization*, Jenny Brine
4 *International Monetary Fund*, Anne C. M. Salda
5 *The Commonwealth*, Patricia M. Larby and Harry Hannam
6 *The French Secret Services*, Martyn Cornick and Peter Morris
7 *Organization of African Unity*, Gordon Harris
8 *North Atlantic Treaty Organization*, Phil Williams
9 *World Bank*, Anne C. M. Salda
10 *United Nations System*, Jospeh P. Baratta
11 *Organization of American States*, David Sheinin
12 *The British Secret Services*, Philip H. J. Davies
13 *The Israeli Secret Services*, Frank A. Clements